Reading STREET

Grades 3-6

Scott Foresman
Vocabulary
Teacher's Guide and Student Worktext

PEARSON

Glenview, Illinois
Boston, Massachusetts
Chandler, Arizona
Upper Saddle River, New Jersey

ISBN-13: 978-0-328-47833-0
ISBN-10:   0-328-47833-4
9 10 V016 18 17 16 15 14 13

Reading Street Response to Intervention Kit

Program Overview

The *Reading Street Response to Intervention Kit* provides targeted instruction in core English-Language Arts standards for Grades K to 2 in each of the five critical areas of reading instruction: phonemic awareness, phonics and decoding, fluency, vocabulary, and comprehension. The Kit, designed for small-group or one-on-one instruction, includes lessons on core skills, allowing teachers to focus on the skills students need most and help them make rapid progress to achieve grade-level proficiency.

Each lesson includes three customized mini-lessons differentiated for the following reading and skill levels:

Mini-Lesson 1: Level 1 (Grades K–1)

Mini-Lesson 2: Level 2 (Grades 2–3)

Mini-Lesson 3: Level 3 (Grades 4–5)

For additional information about the *Reading Street Response to Intervention Kit*, see "How to Use This Kit" in the RTI Kit Implementation Guide.

Vocabulary Teacher's Guide and Student Worktext

The Teacher's Guide portion includes

- three-tiered, differentiated lessons for 20–25 core skills and strategies
- a routine, activities, and 16–20 word lists for teaching high-frequency words
- reinforcement for the strategies and routines used in the core program
- vocabulary strategies embedded in each vocabulary skill lesson

The Student Worktext portion includes

- additional skills practice
- word cards and context sentences
- School+Home activities on every page

Lesson Features

- **Set the scene** introduces the lesson topic to students.
- **Objectives** identify the instructional objectives for students.
- **Materials** list the Worktext components and additional supporting materials for the lesson.
- **Direct teaching** is provided through explicit teacher modeling and consistent routines.
- **Mini-Lessons** are provided for differentiated instruction.
- **Guided practice** for each mini-lesson consists of ample group practice with multiple response opportunities.
- **Independent practice (On Their Own)** allows students to apply skills independently.
- **If…/then…** provides teachers with specific activities for reinforcing skills.

Table of Contents
Vocabulary

Vocabulary
Teacher's Guide

Vocabulary Lesson 1
High-Frequency Words

This lesson demonstrates the instruction you will use for Word Lists 2–16.

Objectives:

- Use and recognize high-frequency words in sentences.
- Learn the correct spellings and pronunciations of high-frequency words.

MATERIALS

Worktext pp. 2–3
Routine Card 8

WORD LIST 1

come	said
help	what
little	where
many	your

Set the scene — Introduce to students the concept of high-frequency words. You know that putting letters together makes words. We learn to read some words by saying the sounds that the letters spell. Other words we have to learn by just remembering the letters. Today we're going to learn words by remembering their letters.

Model and teach — Write the word *where*. This is a word that I need to remember the letters for. To help me remember the word, I will say it and spell it. This word is *where*. It has five letters. Using the word in a sentence helps me understand it: *Where are you going after school?*

1 Introduce the Words

Routine Nondecodable Words

1 Say and Spell Some words we have to learn by remembering the letters rather than sounding them out. We will say and spell the words to learn them. Write the word *your*. This is the word *your*. The letters in *your* are *y-o-u-r, your*. What are the letters in *your*? Have students say and spell the word, first with you and then without you.

2 Demonstrate Meaning Tell me a sentence using this word. Encourage students to look up the words in a dictionary as needed.

If... students have trouble using the word in a sentence,
then... identify the word and model how to use it in a sentence: The word is *your*. A sentence with *your* is *I like your hat.* Have students repeat the sentence.

3 Write Point to the word *your*. Now you write *your*. What letters are in *your*? Have students confirm their spelling by comparing it to what you've written.

If... students have difficulty writing the word,
then... point to each letter in the word, name it, and allow time for students to write it.

Repeat this routine with the words *come, help, little, many, said, what,* and *where*.

2 Read Words

Worktext pp. 2–41

Guide Practice Use the Worktext pages to help students recognize high-frequency words in sentences. Now we will read sentences that have today's words in them. Read the first word and its sentence aloud.

Point to the first word. What's the word? Allow three seconds for students to identify each word before they read it aloud. For decodable words, remind students that these are words that have sounds they must blend. Continue in this way with each word.

Second Reading Then have students read the whole sentence at a natural pace as they point to each word. Have students cut apart the cards and keep them for word reading practice.

If... students cannot read a word,
then... model how to say and spell the high-frequency words (Routine Card 8) and use sound-by-sound blending (Routine Card 1) for decodable words.

3 More Practice

On Their Own Use Activity 1, p. T•8, for more practice with the lesson's high-frequency words. After the group has successfully completed the activity, point to the words in random order and ask individuals to read them.

High-Frequency Word Activities

Activity 1

Find the Missing Word   Give each student a set of high-frequency word cards. Say sentences that are missing one of the high-frequency words. Have students hold up the missing word, say it and spell it, and then as a group repeat the completed sentence.

Activity 2

Write a word   Have students work in pairs. Give each pair a set of word cards, a book, pencils, and paper. Have pairs set up the book between them as a barrier. Partner A picks a word card and spells the word, one letter at a time. Partner B writes the letters. When the word has been spelled, Partner B reads the word. Then partners switch roles.

Activity 3

Word Bingo   Create a simple Bingo Card with nine boxes, three down and three across. For each student, write the high-frequency words in random order on copies of the Bingo Card. If there are fewer than nine words, designate extra spaces as "free" spaces. Say a high-frequency word. Have students find the word on their cards and place a marker on it. When students get Bingo, have them read all the winning words aloud.

Activity 4

Guess the Word   Give each student a set of high-frequency word cards, pencils, and paper. Ask each student to number the paper 1–5. Then give students five clues relating to a high-frequency word from the set. Clues can include the first letter of the word, the number of letters in the word, a rhyming word, a definition, or a sentence that includes the word. After each clue, ask students to write their guess on the paper. If later clues confirm a student's original guess, he or she will write the same word multiple times.

WORD LIST 2

could	people
food	there
live	together
paper	work

To introduce and practice the words in Word List 2, use:
- Lesson 1, pp. T•6–T•7
- Worktext, pp. 4–5
    - **p. 4** Context Sentences
    - **p. 5** Word Cards
- Activity 2, p. T•8

WORD LIST 3

always	grow
around	house
become	water
family	were

To introduce and practice the words in Word List 3, use:
- Lesson 1, pp. T•6–T•7
- Worktext, pp. 6–7
    - **p. 6** Context Sentences
    - **p. 7** Word Cards
- Activity 3, p. T•8

WORD LIST 4

enough	our
every	own
everything	school
nothing	their

To introduce and practice the words in Word List 4, use:
- Lesson 1, pp. T•6–T•7
- Worktext, pp. 8–9
    - **p. 8** Context Sentences
    - **p. 9** Word Cards
- Activity 4, p. T•8

WORD LIST 5

afraid	friends
again	goodbye
does	know
done	read

To introduce and practice the words in Word List 5, use:
- Lesson 1, pp. T•6–T•7
- Worktext, pp. 10–11
    - **p. 10** Context Sentences
    - **p. 11** Word Cards
- Activity 1, p. T•8

WORD LIST 6

about	surprise
before	won't
right	worry
sign	would

To introduce and practice the words in Word List 6, use:
- Lesson 1, pp. T•6–T•7
- Worktext, pp. 12–13
  - **p. 12** Context Sentences
  - **p. 13** Word Cards
- Activity 2, p. T•8

WORD LIST 7

blue	quickly
green	stood
might	three
pulling	woman

To introduce and practice the words in Word List 7, use:
- Lesson 1, pp. T•6–T•7
- Worktext, pp. 14–15
  - **p. 14** Context Sentences
  - **p. 15** Word Cards
- Activity 3, p. T•8

WORD LIST 8

above	great
colors	once
draw	picture
found	touch

To introduce and practice the words in Word List 8, use:
- Lesson 1, pp. T•6–T•7
- Worktext, pp. 16–17
  - **p. 16** Context Sentences
  - **p. 17** Word Cards
- Activity 4, p. T•8

WORD LIST 9

alone	large
company	surface
five	under
four	whatever

To introduce and practice the words in Word List 9, use:
- Lesson 1, pp. T•6–T•7
- Worktext, pp. 18–19
  - **p. 18** Context Sentences
  - **p. 19** Word Cards
- Activity 1, p. T•8

WORD LIST 10

across	opened
because	remember
laugh	thought
only	took

To introduce and practice the words in Word List 10, use:
- Lesson 1, pp. T•6–T•7
- Worktext, pp. 20–21
  - **p. 20** Context Sentences
  - **p. 21** Word Cards
- Activity 2, p. T•8

WORD LIST 11

among	instead
behind	loved
door	shoes
eyes	toward

To introduce and practice the words in Word List 11, use:
- Lesson 1, pp. T•6–T•7
- Worktext, pp. 22–23
  - **p. 22** Context Sentences
  - **p. 23** Word Cards
- Activity 3, p. T•8

WORD LIST 12

against	heavy
another	none
early	should
goes	today

To introduce and practice the words in Word List 12, use:
- Lesson 1, pp. T•6–T•7
- Worktext, pp. 24–25
  - **p. 24** Context Sentences
  - **p. 25** Word Cards
- Activity 4, p. T•8

WORD LIST 13

answered	different
beautiful	learn
built	science
country	through

To introduce and practice the words in Word List 13, use:
- Lesson 1, pp. T•6–T•7
- Worktext, pp. 26–27
  - **p. 26** Context Sentences
  - **p. 27** Word Cards
- Activity 1, p. T•8

WORD LIST 14

build	move
couldn't	someone
everywhere	somewhere
machines	world

To introduce and practice the words in Word List 14, use:
- Lesson 1, pp. T•6–T•7
- Worktext, pp. 28–29
    - **p. 28** Context Sentences
    - **p. 29** Word Cards
- Activity 2, p. T•8

WORD LIST 15

animals	listen
break	often
gone	pieces
heard	though

To introduce and practice the words in Word List 15, use:
- Lesson 1, pp. T•6–T•7
- Worktext, pp. 30–31
    - **p. 30** Context Sentences
    - **p. 31** Word Cards
- Activity 3, p. T•8

WORD LIST 16

bought	minute
brought	whole
either	worst
everybody	you're

To introduce and practice the words in Word List 16, use:
- Lesson 1, pp. T•6–T•7
- Worktext, pp. 32–33
    - **p. 32** Context Sentences
    - **p. 33** Word Cards
- Activity 4, p. T•8

WORD LIST 17

been	guess
believe	half
caught	neighbor
finally	tomorrow

To introduce and practice the words in Word List 17, use:
- Lesson 1, pp. T•6–T•7
- Worktext, pp. 34–35
  - **p. 34** Context Sentences
  - **p. 35** Word Cards
- Activity 1, p. T•8

WORD LIST 18

buy	money
clothes	question
daughters	taught
hours	youngest

To introduce and practice the words in Word List 18, use:
- Lesson 1, pp. T•6–T•7
- Worktext, pp. 36–37
  - **p. 36** Context Sentences
  - **p. 37** Word Cards
- Activity 2, p. T•8

WORD LIST 19

between	mountains
covered	promised
following	second
measure	sometimes

To introduce and practice the words in Word List 19, use:
- Lesson 1, pp. T•6–T•7
- Worktext, pp. 38–39
  - **p. 38** Context Sentences
  - **p. 39** Word Cards
- Activity 3, p. T•8

WORD LIST 20

beginning	sentence
decided	straight
important	thousands
seemed	usually

To introduce and practice the words in Word List 20, use:
- Lesson 1, pp. T•6–T•7
- Worktext, pp. 26–27
  - **p. 40** Context Sentences
  - **p. 41** Word Cards
- Activity 4, p. T•8

Vocabulary Lesson 2
Compound Words

Objectives:
- Understand how to read compound words.
- Use and recognize compound words in sentences.

MATERIALS

Worktext pp. 42–44

Set the scene Introduce to students the concept of compound words. Today we are going to learn about words called *compound words*. A *compound word* is made of two small words put together. We use and hear compound words every day. *Chalkboard, airplane,* and *newspaper* are all compound words.

Model and teach Model reading a compound word by looking at the small words separately. Write *daylight.* This is the compound word *daylight.* When I read the word *daylight,* I first figure out the small word I see at the beginning. Cover *light* with your hand. The first small word in *daylight* is *day.* Then I read the second word. Cover *day.* The second small word is *light.* Then I read the two parts together. Run your hand under both parts of the word as you read: *day, light, daylight.*

Then teach students to look at the meanings of small words for clues to the meanings of compound words. We just learned that *daylight* is made of two words: *day* and *light.* Like many compound words, I can figure out the meaning of *daylight* by looking at its two parts. I know that the word *day* means the time when the sun is out. *Light* is a word for brightness. The word *daylight* must mean the light of day. A sentence with this word is *The soccer field is not lit, so we have to play in the daylight.* If students cannot figure out the meaning of a compound word by looking at its parts, encourage students to look it up in a dictionary as needed.

Follow the same procedure with *moonlight* and *firelight.* Ask students what other compound words they can think of that include the word *light.*

Remind students that...
- a compound word is a word made of two words.
- breaking apart a compound word can help explain the word's meaning.

Word List

airplane	popcorn
backpack	raincoat
bedtime	rowboat
goldfish	sandbox
playpen	teapot

Guide Practice

Use the Word List to continue teaching about compound words. Write *raincoat.* This is the word *raincoat.* Ask students to repeat the word.

- What two small words do you hear in the word *raincoat*? (*rain* and *coat*)

- I want to put a line in the word *raincoat* to separate the two words. Where does the word *rain* end and *coat* begin? (after the *n* and before the *c*) Draw a line between *rain* and *coat.*
- What is a raincoat? (a coat you wear in the rain)
- What is a sentence that uses this word? (Possible response: Jessica has a yellow raincoat.)

Follow the same procedure with the remaining words from the Word List.

If... students have difficulty separating the compound words into two words,

then... write each small word separately and help students read those words first.

On Their Own For additional practice, ask students to complete Worktext p. 42.

Mini-Lesson 2

Remind students that...
- a compound word is a word made of two words.
- figuring out the small words within compound words makes compound words easier to read.

Word List

basketball	fireworks
chalkboard	grandparent
cupcake	highway
downtown	ladybug
eardrum	postcard

Guide Practice

Use the Word List to continue teaching compound words. Write *postcard*. This is the compound word *postcard*. Let's read the word by looking at each small word separately.

- What is the first small word? (post)
- What is the second small word? (card)

- Now let's read the whole word. Run your hand under the word as the class reads the word aloud.
- What is the meaning of *postcard*? (Possible responses: something you send in the mail; a card with a picture on it)
- How do the words *post* and *card* relate to the word *postcard*? (Possible responses: A postcard is a kind of card; you mail a postcard from a post office.)

Follow the same procedure for the remaining words in the Word List.

If... students cannot determine the small words that make up the compound word,
then... cover the second word and have students read the first word aloud. Reveal the second word in the same way.

On Their Own Ask students to complete Worktext p. 43.

Mini-Lesson 3

Remind students that...
- a compound word is a word made of two words.
- breaking apart a compound word can help explain the word's meaning.

Word List

background	eyelash
ballpoint	runway
bedspread	snapshot
earthquake	stopwatch
downpour	wheelchair

Guide Practice

Use the Word List to continue teaching compound words. Write *wheelchair*. Have children read the word with you. As a group, identify the small words that make up the compound word. Then ask the following questions.

- *Wheelchair* is a word that means what? (Possible responses: a chair that has wheels; something that helps people who cannot walk well)
- What is a sentence that includes this word? (Sample response: My grandpa can move faster than I can in his new wheelchair.)

Follow the same procedure with the remaining words in the Word List. Have children tell the meanings of the words and use them in sentences.

If... students cannot determine the meanings of compound words,
then... help them by telling them the meanings of the small words or by using the words in a sentence.

On Their Own For additional practice with words from the Word List, ask students to complete Worktext p. 44.

Vocabulary Lesson 3
Descriptive Words

Objectives:
- Learn descriptive words.
- Give detailed descriptions.

MATERIALS
Worktext pp. 45–47

Set the scene Introduce to students the concept of descriptive words. We describe things every day. For example, we talk about what we did on the weekend, what we thought about a movie, and what we saw on the way to school or on TV. In order to clearly describe things, we need to give details and use descriptive words.

Model and teach Model giving a detailed description. If I tell you "I had breakfast this morning," it doesn't tell you much about my breakfast. A more detailed description would include what I ate and how it tasted. Listen to this description of my breakfast: *This morning I came downstairs to the smell of hot chocolate and warm toast. I sipped the hot chocolate and felt its warm steam against my face. After spreading raspberry jam on the crispy toast, I scooped my spoon into a juicy grapefruit. It was sour, but the jam was very sweet.*

Explain to children that there are different types of descriptive words. When I talked about my breakfast, I described the temperature of the hot chocolate, how the toast felt, and how the grapefruit tasted. When we describe different things, we use even more kinds of descriptive words. I might describe a noise as *loud, banging,* or *hushed.* Words for textures include *soft, smooth,* and *spiky.* Words for actions can also be descriptive; did you *sprint* to school or *stroll*? Model sprinting and strolling. When I use descriptive words, I try to make whoever is listening feel as if he or she can see, smell, or touch whatever I am describing. Explain to students that they can use a dictionary or thesaurus to look up descriptive words.

 **Mini-Lesson 1**

Remind students that...
- descriptive words help people imagine the things we describe more clearly.
- words for colors are descriptive words.

Word List

blue	pink
brown	purple
dark	red
green	white
light	yellow

Guide Practice
Use the Word List to continue teaching descriptive words. Write *sky, grass, tree,* and *sun* in one column. Write the remaining words in another column. Read the words along with students. Imagine it is a beautiful spring day in a park. Let's talk about what we see. To start our description, we can talk about the colors in the park.

Picture the sky. What does it look like? Now think of a tree you see in the park. What are its colors? How does it feel to the touch?

Encourage students to give a variety of details. Have them use descriptive words other than words for colors. Ask students to describe what they do in the park, who they are with, and what they see and hear.

If... students have difficulty creating detailed descriptions,
then... first ask them to describe objects in the classroom. Ask students to help one another by volunteering descriptive details.

On Their Own For additional practice, ask students to complete Worktext p. 45.

Mini-Lesson 2

Remind students that...
- descriptive words help people imagine the things we describe more clearly.
- words for feelings can be descriptive words.

Word List

above	loud
beneath	quiet
beside	relaxed
eager	shy
grumpy	sudden

Guide Practice
Use the Word List to continue teaching descriptive words. Write *grumpy, eager, relaxed,* and *shy.* Read the words with the class. *Grumpy, eager, relaxed,* and *shy* are words that describe how people feel. Point to *eager.*

- What is this word? (eager)
- What does *eager* mean? (Possible responses: excited, looking forward to something)
- Think of a time when you felt *eager.* When was it? (Answers will vary.)

Continue asking students questions about the time they felt eager. Encourage them to provide lots of details in their descriptions. Repeat this process with the rest of the words. Then use the remaining words to have students describe a sound (*loud, quiet,* or *sudden*) and the placement of an object (*above, beneath,* or *beside*).

If... students have difficulty giving detailed descriptions, **then...** give them prompts, such as *When I feel eager, I tap my toes and talk loudly. What do you do when you feel eager?*

On Their Own Have students complete Worktext p. 46 for additional practice with descriptive words.

Mini-Lesson 3

Remind students that...
- *describing* is painting a picture with words.
- knowing descriptive words can help us give better descriptions.

Word List

amazing	fierce
cautious	lively
charming	murky
dangerous	peculiar
enormous	shimmering

Guide Practice
Use the Word List to continue teaching the importance of using descriptive words. Write *glance* and *glare.* These are the words *glance* and *glare.* Both words describe ways of looking at something, but we use the words to talk about different situations. Point to the word *glance.*

- What is this word? (glance)
- What does *glance* mean? (to look at something quickly)
- How is glancing at something different than glaring at it? (Sample response: When you glare at something, you are probably angry.)

Ask students to describe in detail a real or imaginary situation in which they glance or glare at something. Repeat this process for the words *shimmering* and *murky, slouch* and *crouch, holler* and *remark,* or *amazing* and *peculiar.*

If... students have difficulty using descriptive words from the Word List, **then...** define each word and model using it in a description.

On Their Own For additional practice with words from the Word List, ask students to complete Worktext p. 47.

Vocabulary Lesson 4
Sort Words

Objectives:
- Identify word groups within a larger group of words.
- Sort words into multiple categories.

MATERIALS

Worktext pp. 48–50

Set the scene Introduce the concept of sorting words to students. Putting words into groups helps us see how the words are alike and not alike. Sorting words also helps us learn words that are like each other in some way.

Model and teach Write the following words: *delight*, *scare*, *bother*, *amuse*, *annoy*, and *frighten*. Read the words aloud. All of the words in this list describe ways we react to things. If your little brother won't leave you alone, you might react by being *annoyed*. If you hear a strange noise in your house, you might react by being *scared*. I know what *annoy* and *scare* mean, but I am not sure about some of the other words' meanings. Sorting these words into groups will help me think about how the words are similar to or different from each other.

Model sorting the word group into smaller groups. First I will look at a word and think what I know about it. This is the word *delight*. I know that when something is *delightful* it makes people happy. Now I will look at the rest of the list for another word that could go in a group with *delight*. This is the word *bother*. When something *bothers* me, it does not make me happy. The next word is *scare*. *Scare* and *delight* do not go in the same group. The next word in the list is *amuse*. Does something that *amuses* me also make me happy? The answer is yes, so these words can go together. Write *amuse* next to *delight*.

Follow the same procedure to sort the rest of the words into groups: *bother* with *annoy* and *scare* with *frighten*. Explain to students that they can use a dictionary to confirm their groupings.

Mini-Lesson 1

Remind students that...
- sorting words into groups helps us see how words are alike.
- the same group of words can be sorted in different ways.

Word List

breakfast	snow
dinner	spring
heat	summer
lunch	wind
rain	winter

Guide Practice

Use the Word List to continue teaching students how to sort words. Write *snow, summer, wind, rain, spring, heat,* and *winter*. Read the words along with students.

- Out of these words, what is one group we can form? (Possible response: seasons and weather)

- Which words go in the "seasons and weather" group? (winter, spring, summer) Invite a student to circle or rewrite the words.
- What are the remaining words? (rain, snow, heat, wind)
- How can these words go in a group together? What is the name of that group? (words for weather)
- Now let's think of a different way to sort the words. What word goes with "winter" that is not a season? (snow) Ask children to continue sorting the words using this new method of grouping.

If... students have difficulty sorting the words,
then... ask them questions about the members of the group so they can see what they have in common.

On Their Own For additional practice, ask students to complete Worktext p. 48.

Mini-Lesson 2

Remind students that...
- sorting words into groups helps us see how words are alike.
- sorting words can help us learn new words.

Word List

creek	island
desert	mountain
field	ocean
forest	river
hill	valley

Guide Practice

Guide students as they sort words from the Word List into groups. Write *ocean, desert, mountain, hill, river, creek,* and *field.* Read the words aloud with the class. Then inform students that all the words are names for landforms, or features of the earth's surface. Point to *ocean.*

- What is this word? (ocean)
- Can any other words go in a group with the word *ocean*? (yes) Which word? (river)
- Why can the words *ocean* and *river* be grouped together? (Possible response: They both name landforms that are bodies of water.)
- What other word can go in this group? (creek)
- Now we have two groups: "landforms that are bodies of water" and "landforms that are not bodies of water." Let's try sorting the words into even smaller groups.

Guide students to group words for flat landforms (*field* and *desert*) and words for raised landforms (*mountain* and *hill*).

If... students have difficulty sorting words,
then... provide the definition of each word, stressing the similarities between like words.

On Their Own Have students complete Worktext p. 49.

Mini-Lesson 3

Remind students that...
- sorting words into groups helps us see how words relate to each other.
- sorting words helps us learn new words.

Word List

alligator	mammal
antelope	minnow
cobra	reptile
cougar	salmon

Guide Practice

Help students find the word groups within the Word List. Write *mammal, fish,* and *reptile* in one column, and write the remaining words in another column. These are three of the groups that scientists use to classify animals. Today we are going to put some words for animals into these groups.

- *Reptiles* are cold-blooded animals with scaly skin. Which words belong in the *reptile* group? (cobra and alligator)
- Mammals are warm-blooded. Most mammals live on land. Which animals belong to this land group? (cougar and antelope)
- Which words go in the *fish* group? (salmon and minnow)

Once students have sorted the words, have them brainstorm other animals that fit in the groups. Write down students' responses.

If... students have difficulty sorting the words,
then... help them look up the various names for animals in a dictionary.

On Their Own For additional practice sorting words, ask students to complete Worktext p. 50.

Vocabulary Lesson 5
Antonyms

Objectives:
- Antonyms are words for opposites.
- Learning words for opposites helps us remember the meanings of words.

MATERIALS

Worktext pp. 51–53

Set the scene

Introduce to students the concept of antonyms. Words for opposites are called *antonyms*. For example, *up* and *down* are antonyms. *Fast* and *slow* are antonyms. Knowing that a word is an antonym, or the opposite, of another word is a good way to remember the meaning of both words. Today we are going to learn more antonyms.

Model and teach

Write the words *afraid, clean, easy, fearless, hard,* and *dirty.* Then read the words aloud. All of these words have an opposite, or antonym, in the list. To match them, I will read each word and think about its meaning. Then I will look for a word in the list that means the opposite. Point to the word *afraid.* This is the word *afraid.* When I am *afraid* of something, I am scared of it. The opposite of *afraid* is *unafraid.* I am going to look for a word in the list that means *unafraid.* The next two words are *clean* and *easy.* Neither of these words is the opposite of *afraid.* The word *fearless* means "without fear." Someone who is fearless is unafraid, so *fearless* and *afraid* are antonyms. A sentence with these words is *The fearless warrior was not afraid of the enemy.* Write *fearless* next to *afraid.*

Follow the same procedure to match *clean* to *dirty* and *hard* to *easy.* After discussing the meaning of each word and its antonym, place the words next to each other. Offer example sentences that include both words in the antonym pairs. For example, *Alicia's car was clean and sparkled, but Becky's car was so dirty you could barely see out the windows.* Explain to students that a thesaurus is a book of synonyms and antonyms. Refer to Lesson 23 on pp. 56–57 as needed.

Mini-Lesson 1

Remind students that...
- antonyms are words for opposites.
- knowing antonyms helps us remember the meanings of words.

Word List

bad	left
cold	long
good	right
hot	short
huge	tiny

Guide Practice

Use the Word List to continue teaching antonyms. Write *hot, left, right, tiny, cold,* and *huge.* Read the words along with students. Point to the word *hot.*

- What is this word? (hot)

- The antonym of *hot* is in the Word List. Which word is it? (cold) Invite a student to circle the antonyms or rewrite the words next to each other.
- What is a sentence that uses both the word *hot* and the word *cold*? (Possible response: My drink was too hot, so I put cold ice cubes into it.)

Repeat the same procedure for the remaining antonym pairs, *left* with *right* and *tiny* with *huge.* For each pair of words, ask students to define the antonyms and use the words in sentences.

If... students do not understand how words are opposite, **then...** give multiple examples of each word. For *left* and *right,* show students that no matter which way you look, *left* and *right* are on opposite sides of your body.

On Their Own For additional practice, ask students to complete Worktext p. 51.

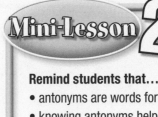

Mini-Lesson 2

Remind students that...
- antonyms are words for opposites.
- knowing antonyms helps us remember the meanings of words.

Word List

answer	fix
arrive	float
begin	leave
break	question
finish	sink

Guide Practice

Guide students as they look for antonym pairs within the Word List. Write the words and read them aloud with the class. Point to the word *arrive*. This is the word *arrive*. Think about this word and look for its opposite, or antonym, in the list of words.

- What is a sentence with the word *arrive*? (Possible response: We will arrive in Chicago at six o'clock.)
- In this sentence, what does *arrive* mean? (Possible response: to get there, to show up)
- When you do the opposite of *arrive*, what do you do? (Possible response: go away from)
- What word in the list means the opposite of *arrive*? (leave)
- Think of the example sentence. Is leaving Chicago the opposite of arriving in Chicago? (yes) Now we know that *arrive* and *leave* are antonyms.

Follow this procedure for the remaining words in the Word List.

If... students have difficulty understanding the relationship between antonyms,
then... provide familiar examples that go along with each word.

On Their Own Have students complete Worktext p. 52.

Mini-Lesson 3

Remind students that...
- antonyms are words for opposites.
- knowing antonyms helps us learn new words.

Word List

ancient	future
careless	history
cautious	loser
champion	modern
dawn	sundown

Guide Practice

Use the Word List to continue teaching antonyms. Write *ancient, future, modern, dawn, sundown,* and *history.* Read the list along with students, helping students read and define difficult words. Point to the word *ancient.* This is the word *ancient.* Let's look for the antonym of this word.

- When you think of the word *ancient,* what do you think of? (Possible responses: history, artifacts, structures such as the pyramids)
- What does *ancient* mean? (very old)
- Let's read through the words again and decide which word is an antonym of *ancient.*

Guide students to see that *modern* is the antonym of *ancient.* Point out that even though the words *history* and *ancient* are related, they are not antonyms. Antonyms are words with opposite, not similar, meanings. Follow the same procedure with the rest of the antonym pairs.

If... students have difficulty identifying antonyms,
then... be sure that students know the meaning of each word.

On Their Own For additional practice with the antonyms from the Word List, ask students to complete Worktext p. 53.

Vocabulary Lesson 6
Greek/Latin Affixes

Objectives:
- Students learn Greek and Latin affixes.
- Students look for Greek and Latin affixes when attempting to learn new words.

MATERIALS
Worktext pp. 54–56

Set the scene Introduce to students the concept of Greek and Latin affixes. Many words have a word part called a *prefix* added to the beginning or a word part called a *suffix* added to the end. In the English language, we use many word parts that come from older languages, especially Latin and Greek. Since so many English words have Greek and Latin word parts, learning the meanings of those word parts can help us learn new words.

Model and teach Model using knowledge of word parts to figure out the meaning of a new word. Write the words *bicycle, bimonthly,* and *bilingual.* All of these words start with the prefix *bi-,* which means "two." Point to the word *bicycle.* One way I remember this prefix is by thinking of the word *bicycle.* I know that a bicycle has two wheels. Write *Laura is bilingual. She speaks both English and Spanish.* Read the sentences aloud. I do not know the meaning of the word *bilingual,* so I am going to look at its word parts and the sentences around the word for clues. Since the word *bilingual* starts with the prefix *bi-,* I know the word has something to do with "two." However, I still don't know what *lingual* means. Now I will look at the other sentence. If Laura speaks both English and Spanish, that means she speaks two languages. Since I know that *bi-* means two, the word *bilingual* must be a word for someone who speaks two languages. If I am still unsure of the meaning, I can look it up in a dictionary.

Mini-Lesson 1

Remind students that...
- prefixes come before a word and change the meaning of the word.
- learning Greek and Latin prefixes helps us learn new words.

Word List
bicycle	semicircle
biweekly	triangle
hemisphere	tricycle
monotonous	unicycle
monotone	uniform

Guide Practice
Use the Word List to continue teaching Greek and Latin affixes. Write *mono* and *uni.* Read the prefixes aloud. *Mono* is Greek, and *uni* is Latin, but both prefixes mean "one." Talk in a monotone voice. If I talk like this in one tone, I am talking in a *monotone* voice. It is *monotonous.* Write *unicycle.*

- You know that a *bicycle* has two wheels. How many wheels do you think a *unicycle* has? **(one)**
- What are some other words you can think of that start with *mono* or *uni*? **(Possible responses: monopoly, monorail, unanimous, uniform, unite)**

Repeat the same procedure to show students that *bi* means "two," *tri* means "three," and *hemi* and *semi* mean "half."

If... students have difficulty giving examples of words with Greek and Latin prefixes,

then... give examples from the Word List, and ask students to provide the definitions.

On Their Own For additional practice, ask students to complete Worktext p. 54.

Mini-Lesson 2

Remind students that...
- prefixes come before a word and change the meaning of the word.
- learning Greek and Latin prefixes helps us learn new words.

Word List

antifreeze	interview
antiwar	submarine
copilot	subzero
coworker	superman
interstate	superstar

Guide Practice

Use the Word List to teach more Greek and Latin prefixes. For each pair of words with the same prefix, such as *copilot* and *coworker,* write the words and read them with students. Ask students: What is a sentence that uses the first word? What is a sentence that uses the second word? From the sentences, what do you think these words mean? What do the words have in common?

Guide students to figure out the meaning of each Greek or Latin prefix: *co-* means "together"; *anti-* means "against"; *inter-* means "between"; *sub-* means "under or less than"; and *super-* means "over or more than."

If... students have difficulty determining the meanings of Greek and Latin prefixes,

then... define example words using the prefix's meaning. For example, *An interstate is a road between two states. An interview is a talk between two or more people.*

On Their Own Have students complete Worktext p. 55.

Mini-Lesson 3

Remind students that...
- a suffix comes after a word and changes the meaning of a word.
- learning Greek and Latin suffixes helps us learn new words.

Word List

artist	ecology
biologist	journalist
biology	novelist
dentist	zoologist
ecologist	zoology

Guide Practice

Use the Word List to guide practice with the Greek suffixes *-logist, -ist,* and *-logy.* Write the three suffixes. Then write *biologist* and *biology.*

- What does the sentence *A biologist studies biology* tell you about the words *biologist* and *biology*? (Possible responses: A biologist is a person who studies; biology is the subject the person studies.)
- The suffixes *-logist* and *-ist* mean "one who practices." Words with these suffixes are words for people. A biologist is a person who studies living things. The suffix *-logy* means "study or science of." Biology is the study of living things. Now that you know these suffixes, how would you define *ecologist* and *ecology*?

Follow this procedure for the remaining words in the Word List.

If... students have difficulty understanding the words from the Word List,

then... make sure they understand that some suffixes are not attached to entire base words. For example, a *dentist* is not someone who practices "dent." Help students understand roots from the Word List that are not entire words.

On Their Own Have students complete Worktext p. 56.

Vocabulary Lesson 7
Greek/Latin Roots

Objectives:
- Recognize Greek and Latin roots and understand their meanings.
- Use Greek and Latin roots to learn the meanings of new words.

MATERIALS
Worktext pp. 57–59

Set the scene Introduce to students the concept of Greek and Latin roots. When you come across a word that is unfamiliar, it is helpful to look for a root, or word part within the word, that you know. Since many English words have Greek or Latin roots, knowing the meanings of these roots will help you figure out the meanings of new words.

Model and teach Teach students how to use a Greek or Latin root to figure out the meaning of an unfamiliar word. Write the sentence *Jack wore thermal socks under his boots.* Underline *thermal* and read the sentence aloud. In this sentence, I do not know what the word *thermal* means. To figure out the word, I am going to look for any familiar roots. Then I will think of other words I know that have the same root. Using those words as clues, I will try to determine the meaning of *thermal.* Finally, I will check to see if the meaning that I figured out makes sense in the sentence.

Model using the Greek root *therm* to figure out the meaning of *thermal.* Circle *therm.* I know other words that start with these letters. *Thermometer, thermos,* and *thermostat* all have the Greek root *therm.* A *thermometer* measures heat. A *thermostat* controls the temperature inside my house. I put drinks like tea and coffee in a *thermos* to keep them hot. The root *therm* must mean "heat." *Thermal* socks must be socks that keep feet warm. This meaning makes sense in the sentence *Jack wore thermal socks under his boots.*

Explain to students that they can use a dictionary to confirm the meanings of the words.

Remind students that...
- many words have Greek and Latin roots.
- learning Greek and Latin roots helps us learn new words.

Word List
telephone	attract
telescope	thermometer
television	thermos
telegram	astronaut
traction	astronomy

Guide Practice
Use the Word List to continue teaching Greek and Latin roots. Write *tele* and read the root aloud. The Greek root *tele* means "distant" or "far." You use a *telephone* to talk to someone who is far away. Let's think of more words that begin with *tele.*

- I am thinking of something that helps people see things that are very far away, like planets and stars. What is it? (telescope)
- Now I am thinking of something that people watch to see things that are happening far away. What is it? (television)

Ask pairs of students to use a dictionary and find more words that begin with *tele* (such as *telegraph* and *televise*). Have them make each other guess the words. Repeat this process for the remaining words in the Word List. Tell students that *tract* means "pull," and *astr* means "star."

If... students have difficulty thinking of words with Greek roots,

then... give examples from the Word List, and ask students to provide the definitions.

On Their Own For additional practice, ask students to complete Worktext p. 57.

Mini-Lesson 2

Remind students that...
- many English words have Greek or Latin roots.
- learning Greek and Latin roots helps us learn new words.

Word List

describe	scribble
export	scribe
import	script
portable	transcript
porter	transport

Guide Practice

Use the Word List to teach more Greek and Latin roots. Write *scrib* and *script*. The Latin roots *scrib* and *script* have to do with writing. *Scrib* means "write," and *script* means "written." Let's figure out words with the roots *scrib* and *script*.

- Listen to this sentence: *In ancient Egypt, scribes kept records and were a part of the royal court.* Which word includes the root *scrib*? (scribe) Write *scribe*.
- What does the sentence tell you about scribes? (Possible response: Scribes were people who lived in ancient Egypt.)
- What does the root *scrib* tell you about *scribe*? (It has something to do with writing.) What do you think a *scribe* does? (writes)

Follow the same procedure with other words from the Word List. Tell students that the Latin root *port* means "carry."

If... students have difficulty determining the meanings of words with Latin roots,
then... provide leading prompts, such as *If something is portable, can you carry it?*

On Their Own Have students complete Worktext p. 58.

Mini-Lesson 3

Remind students that...
- many English words have Greek or Latin roots.
- learning roots helps us learn new words.

Word List

dictate	interrupt
diction	rupture
predict	spectacle
eruption	spectator
inspect	verdict

Guide Practice

Use the Word List to guide practice with the Latin roots. Write *rupt, spect,* and *dict*. Tell students that *rupt* means "break," *spect* means "see," and *dict* means "speak." Write *The spectators cheered at the end of the game.* Underline *spectators*.

- Which Latin root does this word contain? (spect) Circle *spect*.
- What other words do you know with the root *spect*? (Possible responses: *inspect, spectacular*) What does *spect* mean? (see)
- What does the sentence tell you about the word *spectator*? (Possible response: Spectators are people who are seeing a game.)
- Use clues from the sentence to figure out what you know about the root *spect*. What do you think *spectator* means? (someone who sees or watches something)

Follow the same procedure with other words from the Word List.

If... students have difficulty determining words' Latin roots,
then... group together words with the same root. Discuss with students how the root's meaning relates to each word.

On Their Own Have students complete Worktext p. 59.

Vocabulary Lesson 8
Homonyms

Objectives:
- Learn that homonyms look and sound the same but have different meanings.
- Use and recognize homonyms.

MATERIALS
Worktext pp. 60–62

Set the scene

Introduce to students the concept of homonyms. Some words look and sound the same but have different meanings. These words are called *homonyms*. Today we are going to talk about homonyms and learn how to figure out which meaning of a homonym is being used in a sentence.

Model and teach

Give students examples of homonyms. The word *lie* means different things at different times. Sometimes *lie* means to be in a flat position. For example, *Every night I lie in bed. Lie* can also mean to make a statement that is untrue. For example, *Jack's grandma told him never to lie.*

Model how to use substitution to determine the meaning of a homonym in a sentence.

To figure out the meaning of a homonym in a sentence, I can replace the word with the meanings I know and see if the sentence makes sense. Write *Molly was the last person in line.* Underline *last.* I know that the word *last* has more than one meaning. *Last* means "final." It can also mean "go on or continue." If I say *Molly was the go on person in line,* the sentence does not make sense. However, the sentence *Molly was the final person in line* does make sense. In this sentence, *last* means "final." Explain to students that context clues can help them figure out which meaning to use. They can also use a dictionary to confirm which meaning to use.

Mini-Lesson 1

Remind students that...
- homonyms look and sound the same but have different meanings.
- clue words can help us figure out homonyms' meanings.

Word List

calf	left
duck	pen
fair	ray
fan	ring
fly	row

Guide Practice

Use the Word List to continue teaching homonyms. Write *row.* The word *row* has more than one meaning. What are some meanings of the word *row*? (Possible responses: paddle a boat, a line of people or objects) Listen to this sentence: *There was a row of cars as far as the eye*

could see. Which meaning of *row* makes sense? (a line) How do you know this meaning is correct? (Possible response: The meaning "row a boat" does not make sense.)

Follow the same procedure using other words from the Word List. Possible example sentences include: *Lee saw a brown <u>duck</u> on the lake. Please be <u>fair</u> and wait for your turn. We saw a cow and a <u>calf</u> at the farm.*

If... students have difficulty thinking of multiple meanings for each word,
then... provide multiple example sentences, and ask students to talk about how the meanings differ between the sentences.

On Their Own For additional practice, ask students to complete Worktext p. 60.

Remind students that...

• *homonyms* mean different things at different times.

• looking at clues in sentences can help us determine the meanings of homonyms.

Word List

band	lap
bill	match
bow	pitcher
cape	peep
key	pupil

Guide Practice

Use words from the Word List to guide practice with more homonyms. Write *The eye doctor looked into Lauren's pupil.* Underline *pupil.* Read the sentence aloud with students.

• What are the two meanings of the word *pupil*? (student and part of the eye)

• What words are clues to the meaning of the word *pupil* in this sentence? (Possible responses: eye, doctor, looked into) Circle words that students identify.

• Based on the clues, what do you think *pupil* means in this sentence? (part of the eye)

• What is a sentence that uses the other meaning of *pupil*? (Possible response: Every pupil sat still and listened to the teacher.)

Follow the same procedure using other words from the Word List. Encourage students to think of as many meanings as possible for each homonym.

If... students have difficulty identifying clues within sentences,

then... provide one clue, and ask students to name additional clues that support the same meaning.

On Their Own Have students complete Worktext p. 61.

Remind students that...

• homonyms look and sound the same but have different meanings.

• looking at clues in sentences can help us determine the meanings of homonyms.

Word List

bass	loom
bug	mount
forge	peer
graze	plot
groom	quiver

Guide Practice

Use the Word List to guide practice with homonyms. Write *Sir Edmund Hilary was the first person to climb Mount Everest.* Below this sentence, write *Please mount the painting on this wall.* Finally, write *The cowboy can mount his horse in seconds.*

• What homonym do these three sentences share? (mount)

• What are some meanings of the word *mount*? (Possible responses: mountain, to attach to something for support, to be seated on something)

• Does the word *mount* have the same meaning in any of the sentences? (no) Let's look for clue words that will help us figure out the correct meanings.

Guide students as they point out clue words and determine meanings. Circle words or phrases they identify. Follow the same procedure for other homonyms in the Word List. Some words have only two meanings.

If... students have difficulty figuring out the meaning of a word,

then... ask them to look up the word in a dictionary to view all the possible meanings.

On Their Own Have students complete Worktext p. 62.

Multiple-Meaning Words

Objectives:

- Learn multiple-meaning words.
- Use clues in sentences to figure out the meanings of multiple-meaning words.

MATERIALS

Worktext pp. 63–65

Set the scene Introduce to students the concept of multiple-meaning words. Some words mean different things at different times. For example, in the sentence *Each piece of candy costs a quarter,* the word *quarter* means "a coin worth twenty-five cents." In the sentence *Practice starts at a quarter after four,* the word *quarter* means one fourth of an hour, or fifteen minutes. Today we will learn more words that have multiple meanings.

Model and teach Model for students how to look for clues in a sentence to determine the meaning of a multiple-meaning word. When I read a multiple-meaning word in a sentence, first I think of all the meanings for that word that I know. Then I look for clues in the sentence to figure out the correct meaning. If I am not sure, I can substitute meanings into the sentence to see which makes the most sense. Write *Carmen wants to save money to buy a new computer.* Underline *save.* I know that the word *save* has more than one meaning. *Save* can mean "rescue from danger." It can also mean "put aside." In sports, *save* means "prevent someone from scoring." From the sentence, I know that the word *save* describes what Jane wants to do with her money so that she can buy a new computer. Nothing in the sentence talks about a sport or any kind of danger. In this sentence, *save* must mean "put aside." *Jane wants to put aside money to buy a new computer* makes sense. *Jane wants to rescue money to buy a new computer* does not. Explain to students that they can use a dictionary to confirm the meanings of the words.

Remind students that...

- some words have more than one meaning.
- clues in sentences can help us figure out the meanings of multiple-meaning words.

Word List

bank	cap
bark	coat
bat	horn
bed	ring
block	trunk

Guide Practice

Use the Word List to continue teaching multiple-meaning words. Write *ring.* Read the word aloud with students.

- What are some meanings of the word *ring*? (Possible responses: something you wear on your finger, a sound that a bell or a phone makes)

- In the sentence *My sister got a silver ring for her birthday,* which meaning of *ring* makes sense? (something you wear on your finger)
- How do you know that this is the correct meaning of *ring*? (Possible response: A sound cannot be silver.)

Continue in this way with other words from the Word List. Encourage students to think of two or more different meanings for each word.

If... students have difficulty determining the correct meaning,

then... model substituting incorrect meanings into the sentence. For example, *My sister got a silver sound a bell makes for her birthday.*

On Their Own Direct students to complete Worktext p. 63. Assist students in reading any unfamiliar words.

Mini-Lesson 2

Remind students that…
- some words have more than one meaning.
- clues in sentences can help us figure out the meanings of multiple-meaning words.

Word List

beam	feeling
blend	float
break	leaf
clear	patch
company	wear

Guide Practice

Use the Word List to guide practice with multiple-meaning words. Write *company*. Ask students to provide one meaning for the word *company,* such as "guests." Then ask them to use that meaning of the word in a sentence. After students have come up with multiple meanings for the word, write *Joe's dad works for a large company.*

Ask students: Which meaning of the word *company* makes the most sense in this sentence? (a business) What clue words in the sentence helped you figure out the correct meaning? (works for)

Follow the same procedure using other words from the Word List.

If… students have difficulty coming up with multiple meanings of words,

then… provide example sentences with context clues.

On Their Own For additional practice with words from the Word List, have students complete Worktext p. 64.

Mini-Lesson 3

Remind students that…
- words that have more than one meaning are called *multiple-meaning words.*
- clue words in sentences help us determine the meaning of multiple-meaning words.

Word List

blade	file
character	grasp
charm	negative
draft	stall
drill	trace

Guide Practice

Use the words from the Word List to guide practice with multiple-meaning words. Write *Lisa's mom has a stall in the market where she sells apples.* Read the sentence aloud with students.

- Which word in the sentence is a multiple-meaning word? (stall)
- What are some meanings of the word *stall*? (Possible responses: a place to keep a horse, a booth used to sell things, to stop working)
- What do the clues in the sentence tell you about the word? (Possible responses: It's in the market; Lisa's mom sells apples there.)
- Based on these clues, which meaning of *stall* makes the most sense? (a booth or stand used to sell things)

Repeat this process with other words from the Word List. Encourage students to think of multiple meanings for each word.

If… students have difficulty identifying clues within the example sentences,

then… point out one clue and ask students to identify other clues that support the same meaning.

On Their Own With students, read through the sentences on Worktext p. 65 before students complete the page.

Vocabulary Lesson 10
Prefixes *un-, dis-, mis-*

Objectives:
- Learn the prefixes *un-, dis-,* and *mis-*
- Use and recognize words with these prefixes.

MATERIALS
Worktext pp. 66–68

Set the scene Introduce students to the concept of prefixes. Some words have a word part called a *prefix* added to the beginning. Adding a prefix to a word changes the meaning of the word. Today we will learn about the prefixes *un-, dis-,* and *mis-*.

Model and teach Teach students the meanings of the prefix *un-*. Write *un-*. This is the prefix *un-*. The words *unpack, unfold,* and *unafraid* all have this prefix. *Un-* means "not" or "the opposite of." When I see a word that starts with *un-*, first I read the base word. A *base word* is a word without any added word parts. Write *unplug*. Cover up *un-* with your hand. The base word of *unplug* is *plug*. I know a meaning of the word *plug*. My TV and radio have cords that I *plug*, or connect, into the wall to get electricity. Since *un-* means "the opposite of," to *unplug* means "to disconnect, or take out." A sentence with this word is *Please unplug the lamp in the kitchen.*

Use the same procedure to model reading words with the prefixes *dis-* and *mis-*. Inform students that the prefix *dis-* means "the opposite of," and the prefix *mis-* means "wrong" or "bad." Write *disobey* and *misquote*. Read the base words, then the prefixes, and then the entire words. Provide example sentences, such as *Jack's mom said not to* disobey *the babysitter* and *Use a tape recorder so you do not* misquote *the person you are interviewing.* Explain to students that they can use a dictionary as needed to confirm the meanings of the words or to see example sentences that use the words.

Mini-Lesson 1

Remind students that...
- prefixes are word parts added to the beginning of a word.
- the prefix *un-* means "not" or "the opposite of."

Word List
dislike	pin
do	undo
like	unlock
lock	unpin
misuse	use

Guide Practice
Use the Word List to continue teaching the prefixes *un-, dis-,* and *mis-*. Write *unlock*.

- What is the base word of *unlock*? (lock)
- What is a sentence with the word *lock*? (Possible response: Rachel asked Kurt to lock the door.)

- Now look at the word with its prefix. What does *unlock* mean? (the opposite of lock)
- What is a sentence with this word? (Possible response: Use the key to unlock the door.)

Continue in this way with other words from the Word List. For each word, ask students to identify the prefix and the base word. Have them tell the meaning of the word and use it in a sentence.

If... students have difficulty determining the correct meaning,
then... make sure they understand the meaning of the base word.

On Their Own Direct students to complete Worktext p. 66. Remind students of the meaning of each prefix.

 **Mini-Lesson 2**

Remind students that…

- prefixes come before a word and change the meaning of the word.
- some prefixes change a word into its opposite.

Word List

agree	disbelieve
believe	miscopy
copy	misplace
cover	place
disagree	uncover

Guide Practice

Use the Word List to guide practice with the prefixes *un-*, *dis-*, and *mis-*. Write *disagree*. Ask students to identify the prefix (*dis-*) and the base word (*agree*).

- What does *agree* mean? (Possible response: to have the same opinion)

- You know that the prefix *dis-* means "the opposite of." How would you define *disagree*? (Possible responses: the opposite of agree, having different opinions)
- What is a sentence that uses *disagree*? (Possible response: Even best friends sometimes disagree.)

Follow the same procedure using other words from the Word List. Remind students that *un-* means "not" or "the opposite of" and that *mis-* means "wrong" or "bad."

If… students have difficulty providing a meaning of a word with a prefix,

then… have them say the words "not," "do the opposite of," or "do badly" with the base word. For example, *To misplace is to place something where you can't find it.*

On Their Own Ask students to complete Worktext p. 67. Help them read any unfamiliar words on the page.

Mini-Lesson 3

Remind students that…

- prefixes come before words and change the meaning of the word.
- the prefix *dis-* means "the opposite of."

Word List

advantage	mispronounce
aware	pronounce
disadvantage	prove
disprove	respect
disrespect	unaware

Guide Practice

Use the words from the Word List to guide practice with the prefixes *un-*, *dis-*, and *mis-*. Write *disrespect* and read the word aloud with students. Ask them to identify the prefix and the base word.

- What are some ways that you respect someone?

(Possible response: Listen carefully when he or she speaks.)
- How would you define *disrespect* without using the word *respect*? (Possible response: believing someone or something is not important or valuable)
- What are some ways that people show disrespect? (Possible responses: talking impolitely, not respecting a person's feelings or belongings)

Repeat this process with other words from the Word List. For some words, cover the prefix and assist students as they read the base words first.

If… students have difficulty defining words with prefixes,

then… provide example sentences with the base word and the word with the added prefix. Ask students to explain how the words are different.

On Their Own With students, read through the sentences on Worktext p. 68. Ask students to complete the page.

Vocabulary Lesson 11
Prefixes *pre-, re-*

Objectives:
- Learn the prefixes *pre-* and *re-*.
- Use and recognize words with the prefixes *pre-* and *re-*.

MATERIALS

Worktext pp. 69–71

Set the scene Introduce students to the concept of prefixes. Some words have a word part called a *prefix* added to the beginning. Adding a prefix to a word changes the word's meaning. Today we will learn about the prefixes *pre-* and *re-*.

Model and teach Teach students the meanings of the prefixes *pre-* and *re-*. Adding the prefix *pre-* or *re-* to a word can change the word's meaning. The prefix *pre-* means "before." The prefix *re-* means "again." **Write *precut* and *relearn*.** When I see a word that starts with *pre-* or *re-*, I read the base word first. A *base word* is a word without any added word parts. **Cover up *pre-* with your hand.** The word *precut* has the base word *cut* and the prefix *pre-*. **Run your hand under the word parts as you read:** *pre-, cut, precut.* The word *precut* means "cut before." A sentence with this word is *The potato slices were precut and then frozen.*

Continue modeling how to read words with prefixes. Now I am going to read the word *relearn* in the same way. I see that the prefix of *relearn* is *re-*, which means "again." The base word is *learn. Relearn* means "learn again." A sentence with this word is *I used to know all the state capitals, but I have to relearn them for my geography test.*

Write the words *pretest* and *retest.* Explain that students can figure out the meanings of these words by identifying the prefixes *pre-* and *re-* and the base word *test.* Explain to students that they can use a dictionary to confirm the meanings of the words.

Mini-Lesson 1

Remind students that…
- prefixes are word parts added to the beginning of a word.
- the prefix *pre-* means "before" and *re-* means "again."

Word List

preheat	redraw
prepay	rename
preschool	repack
preset	retell
preteen	reuse

Guide Practice

Use the Word List to continue teaching the prefixes *pre-* and *re-*. Write *Preheat the oven for twenty minutes.* Read the sentence aloud, and tell students that the sentence came from instructions on a frozen pizza.

- Which word in this sentence has the prefix *pre-*? (preheat)
- What is the base word of *preheat*? (heat)
- Use the sentence and what you know about prefixes to define *preheat*. ("heat before")
- What are the instructions asking you to do? (heat the oven for twenty minutes before cooking the pizza)

Continue teaching other words from the Word List. For each word, ask students to identify the prefix and the base word. Then have students tell the meaning of the word and use it in a sentence.

If… students have difficulty determining the correct meaning,
then… make sure they understand the meaning of the base word.

On Their Own For additional practice with words from the Word List, direct students to complete Worktext p. 69.

 **Mini-Lesson 2**

Remind students that...
- knowing prefixes can help us figure out the meanings of words.
- the prefix *pre-* means "before" and *re-* means "again."

Word List

precaution	reappear
predate	rediscover
prejudge	rematch
preorder	reorder
preview	replace

Guide Practice

Use the Word List to guide practice with the prefixes *pre-* and *re-*. Write *The store had to reorder more pens.* Below it, write *Justin will preorder the next book in the series.* Read the sentences aloud.

- Which words in these sentences share a base word? (reorder, preorder) What base word do they share? (order)
- Use what you know about prefixes to figure out what *reorder* and *preorder* mean. ("order again" and "order before")
- Do these meanings make sense in the sentences? (yes) Invite students to explain how they know that the meanings make sense. For example, it makes sense to order the next book in a series before it comes out in stores.

Ask students to identify the prefix, base word, and meaning of the other words from the Word List.

If... students have difficulty providing a meaning of a word with a prefix,

then... model saying the word "again" or "before" with the base word.

On Their Own Ask students to complete Worktext p. 70.

Mini-Lesson 3

Remind students that...
- a prefix comes before a word and changes the meaning of the word.
- the prefix *pre-* means "before" and *re-* means "again."

Word List

prehistoric	reattach
preset	rewrite
preprogram	recapture
preseason	recreate
precook	rephrase

Guide Practice

Use the Word List to guide practice with the prefixes *pre-* and *re-*. Write *prehistoric* and read the word aloud. Ask students to identify the prefix and the base word.

- When have you heard the base word *historic*? What do you think it means? (Possible responses: when talking about an event or landmark that is old or will always be remembered in history; old or having to do with history)
- How would you define *prehistoric*? (Possible response: "before history")
- What is a sentence with this word? (Possible response: Dinosaurs lived in prehistoric times.)

Explain that *prehistoric* means "before written history." Follow the same procedure with other words from the Word List. Before asking students to define words and use them in sentences, make sure they understand the meanings of the base words, such as *capture*.

If... students have difficulty defining words with prefixes,
then... provide example sentences with the base word and the entire word. Ask students to explain how the words are different.

On Their Own With students, read through the sentences on Worktext p. 71. Ask students to complete the page.

Vocabulary Lesson 12
Root Words

Objectives:
- Learn how to identify root words.
- Use root words to determine the meanings of words.

MATERIALS

Worktext pp. 72–74

Set the scene

Introduce students to the concept of root words. Many words have word parts added to the beginning, the end, or both. When you read a word with added word parts, try to figure out the root word. A root word, or base word, cannot be broken down into smaller words or word parts.

Model and teach

Model how to find a root word within a longer word. Write *unthinkable.* The word *unthinkable* looks long and is challenging to read. When I read *unthinkable*, first I find the root word by taking away the added word parts. **Cover** *un-* with your hand. I know that *un-* is a prefix, or a word part that goes before a word. *Un-* means "not" or "do the opposite of." **Cross out** *un-.* Once I take away the prefix *un-,* I have the word *thinkable.* Now I see that this word also has a suffix, or a word part added to the end. **Cross out** *-able.* Now I have the root word *think.* The word *unthinkable* has to do with thinking.

Show students ways to figure out the meaning of a word with a familiar root word. After I know the root word, or base word, I can use the added word parts to help me understand the meaning of the whole word. For example, I know that *–able* means "can be," and *un-* means "not." *Unthinkable* means "cannot be thought about." If I do not know the meaning of the word parts, I can look up the whole word in a dictionary. I can also look for clues in a sentence where I see the word. Emphasize to students that looking at word structure, or the different parts of a word, can help them figure out the meaning of unfamiliar words.

Mini-Lesson 1

Remind students that...
- root words are words that cannot be broken down into smaller words or word parts.
- figuring out root words helps us read longer words.

Word List

do	relearn
redo	paint
end	repaint
unending	play
learn	replay

Guide Practice

Use the Word List to guide practice with root words. Write *repainting* and say the sentence *This weekend Jeb and his dad are repainting the garage.* Start with the word ending *-ing.* Ask students to identify the added word parts. Erase or cross out *-ing* and *re-* as appropriate. After crossing out the word parts, ask students if the

word *paint* can be broken down any further or if paint is the root word. The prefix *re-* means "again." Use the prefix, the root word, and clues from the sentence to figure out the meaning of *repainting.*

Continue guiding practice with words from the Word List. After students identify each root word, ask them to use the whole word in a sentence.

If... students have difficulty determining the meaning of the longer words,
then... model using the whole word and the root word alone in sentences. Discuss how the words differ.

On Their Own For additional practice, direct students to complete Worktext p. 72.

Mini-Lesson 2

Remind students that...
- some words have both a prefix and a suffix or word ending.
- a root word cannot be broken down into smaller words or word parts.

Word List

break	unchanged
breakable	correct
center	uncorrected
centered	lock
change	relock

Guide Practice

Use the Word List to guide practice with root words. Write *Even after twenty years, the house was unchanged.* Read the sentence aloud with students. Which word in this sentence has added words parts? Guide students as they identify the root word of *unchanged.* Inform them that *un-*

means "not" or "the opposite of." The ending *-ed* is used with a word to show past tense. Then ask students to define the word *unchanged* and explain why the meaning makes sense in the sentence.

For the remaining words on the Word List, have students identify each root word. Ask them to talk about how the root words relate to the longer words' meanings.

If... students have difficulty determining the meanings of the longer words,
then... explain that sometimes the root word has multiple meanings. For example, *center* means "the middle," but it also means "to move to the middle."

On Their Own Ask students to complete Worktext p. 73. Assist students as they identify root words.

Mini-Lesson 3

Remind students that...
- some words have both a prefix and a suffix or word ending.
- a root word cannot be broken down into smaller words or word parts.

Word List

approach	construction
approachable	educate
connect	educated
disconnect	increase
construct	increasingly

Guide Practice

Use the Word List to guide practice with root words. Write *Mr. Lee's smile and pleasant voice made him seem approachable.* Point to the word *approachable.*

- What root word do you see in this word? (approach) If students have difficulty identifying the root word, help them by covering up *-able* with your hand.
- What does *approach* mean? (Possible response: come near) From the sentence, the added word part, and the root word, what do you think *approachable* means? (Possible response: inviting or able to be go near)

For the remaining words on the Word List, ask students to identify each root word and use it in a sentence. Then talk about how the meanings of the root words relate to the meanings of the longer words.

If... students have difficulty defining words with affixes,
then... tell them the meaning of the prefix, suffix, or word ending attached to the word.

On Their Own For additional practice with words from the Word List, have students complete Worktext p. 74.

Vocabulary Lesson 13
Suffixes *-ful, -less*

Objectives:
- Learn the suffixes *-ful* and *-less*.
- Use the suffixes *-ful* and *-less* to determine words' meanings.

MATERIALS

Worktext pp. 75–77

Set the scene
Introduce students to the concept of suffixes. Suffixes are word parts added to the end of a word to change the word's meaning. Today we will learn about the suffixes *-ful* and *-less.*

Model and teach
Teach students the meanings of the suffixes *-ful* and *-less.* Write *cheerful* and *cheerless.* The suffix *-ful* means "full of." The suffix *-less* means "not having" or "without." To read a word with the suffix *-ful* or *-less,* first I find the base word. Cover *-ful* and *-less* with your hand. *Cheerful* and *cheerless* have the same base word: *cheer.* After I read the base word, I read the base word and the suffix together. Run your hand under the word parts as you read: *cheer, ful, cheerful.*

Show students how knowledge of suffixes can help them learn new words. Knowing the suffixes *-ful* and *-less* can help me learn new words. When I read a word with the suffix *-ful* or *-less* in a sentence, first I look at the base word. Then I say "full of" or "without" before the base word. Finally, I see if that meaning makes sense in the sentence. Write *The cheerful room had yellow walls and big windows to let in the sunshine.* Below the first sentence, write *The black paint and musty smell made the room feel cheerless.* Read the sentences aloud. The base word *cheer* means "a happy feeling." Would a bright yellow room be "full of cheer"? Yes, that meaning makes sense. Would a dark, musty room be "without cheer"? Yes, this meaning makes sense also. Now I know the meanings of *cheerful* and *cheerless.* Emphasize to students that looking at word structure, or the different parts of a word, can help them figure out the meaning of unfamiliar words.

Mini-Lesson 1

Remind students that...
- suffixes are added to the ends of words to change words' meanings.
- the suffix *-ful* means "full of" and the suffix *-less* means "without."

Word List

careful	hopeless
careless	thankful
helpful	thankless
helpless	useful
hopeful	useless

Guide Practice

Use the Word List to guide practice with the suffixes *-ful* and *-less.* Write *hopeful.* Say the sentence: *Though the score was 6–0, Ben was hopeful his team would win the game.* Ask students to identify the base word and the suffix of *hopeful.* Then have them tell the meaning of the

word and say whether or not the meaning makes sense in the sentence.

For the remaining words in the Word List, ask students to identify the base words and suffixes. Then have students tell the meaning of each word and use it in a sentence.

If... students cannot supply a word meaning,
then... review the meaning of the base word to make sure they understand it. Then have them say the words *full* of or *without* before the base word and discuss the new meaning.

On Their Own For additional practice with words from the Word List, ask students to complete Worktext p. 75.

Remind students that...

- the suffix *-ful* means "full of" and the suffix *-less* means "without."
- knowing suffixes can help us learn new words.

Word List

fearful	mindless
fearless	powerful
harmful	powerless
harmless	restful
mindful	restless

Guide Practice

Use the Word List to guide practice with the suffixes *-ful* and *-less*. Write *Lisa wrote a note to thank Mary for her cheerful birthday card.* Underline *cheerful.* Read the sentence aloud with students. Which word in this sentence has the suffix *-ful*? What is the base word of *cheerful*? What is the meaning of *cheerful*? Why does this meaning make sense in the sentence?

For the remaining words in the Word List, have students identify each word's base word and suffix. Then ask them to tell the meaning of each word and use it in a sentence.

If... students have difficulty using the words in sentences that show they understand the meaning of the word,

then... model thinking about the meaning of the word to come up with a sentence like *Erin's family felt fearful that the tornado would pass through their town.*

On Their Own For additional practice with the words from the Word List, have students complete Worktext p. 76.

Mini-Lesson 3

Remind students that...

- the suffix *-ful* means "full of" and the suffix *-less* means "without."
- knowing suffixes can help us learn new words.

Word List

doubtful	graceless
doubtless	meaningful
flavorful	meaningless
flavorless	thoughtful
graceful	thoughtless

Guide Practice

Use the Word List to guide practice with the suffixes *-ful* and *-less*. Write *Liz looked at the sky and asked Amy if they would make it home by dark. Amy looked doubtful.* Read the sentences aloud and point to the word doubtful.

- What base word do you see and hear in the word *doubtful*? (doubt) What does *doubt* mean? (Possible responses: "to be uncertain, to think something may not be true")
- What does *doubtful* mean? (Possible response: "full of doubt")
- Read the sentences again. Why does this meaning make sense? Encourage students to give reasons for their responses.

Continue teaching the words from the Word List. Ask students to identify the base word and suffix of each word. Then ask them to tell the meaning of each word and use it in a sentence.

If... students cannot supply a meaning,
then... review the meaning of the base word.

On Their Own For additional practice with words from the Word List, have students complete Worktext p. 77.

Vocabulary Lesson 14
Suffixes *-ly, -al*

Objectives:
- Learn the suffixes *-ly* and *-al*.
- Use knowledge of suffixes to learn new words.

MATERIALS
Worktext pp. 78–80

Set the scene Review with students the concept of suffixes. Explain that suffixes are word parts added to the end of a word to change the word's meaning and that today they will learn about the suffixes *-ly* and *-al*.

Model and teach Teach students the meanings of the suffixes *-ly* ("in a certain way") and *-al* ("relating to"). Write *quickly* and *arrival.* The suffix *-ly* means "in a certain way." The suffix *-al* means "relating to." To read a word with the suffix *-ly*, first I find the base word. Cover *-ly* with your hand. The base word of *quickly* is *quick. Quickly* means "in a quick way." A sentence with the word *quickly* is *Kate ran quickly to the store.* Cover *-al* with your hand. To find the base word of *arrival,* I have to remember that some words lose their final *e* when a suffix is added. The base word of *arrival* is *arrive.* Write *arrive.* An *arrival* is the time when you arrive, or get to a place. A sentence with *arrival* is *We went to the airport to wait for my uncle's arrival.*

Show students how a knowledge of suffixes can help them learn new words. Knowing the suffixes *-ly* and *-al* can help me learn new words. Write *Leslie quietly shut the door.* Read the sentence aloud. When I read *quietly* in a sentence, first I look at the base word. I see that the base word of *quietly* is *quiet.* I know that the suffix *-ly* means "in a certain way." *Quietly* means "in a quiet way." After I figure out the meaning of the word, I see if the meaning makes sense in the sentence. It makes sense that someone shuts a door in a quiet way. If I am still unsure of the word's meaning, I can look it up in a dictionary. Explain to students that looking at word structure, or the different parts of a word, can help them figure out the meaning of unfamiliar words.

Remind students that...
- suffixes are added to the ends of words to change meaning.
- the suffix *-ly* means "in a certain way" and the suffix *-al* means "relating to."

Word List

accidental	neatly
coastal	nicely
educational	personal
loudly	sadly
musical	softly

Guide Practice
Use the Word List to guide practice. Write *musical.* Say the sentence: *Ms. Dee plays many musical instruments, including guitar and trombone.* Ask students to identify the base word and the suffix of *musical.* Then have them tell the meaning of the word and say whether or not the meaning makes sense in the sentence.

For the remaining words on the Word List, ask students to identify the base words and suffixes. Then have students tell the meaning of each word and use it in a sentence. When teaching words that do not have clear base words, such as *mental, dental,* and *mortal,* provide students with definitions. Explain that some words have Greek or Latin roots. For example, the Latin root *dent* means "teeth."

If... students cannot supply a word meaning of a word ending in *-ly,*
then... have them say *in a _____ way,* using the base word in the blank.

On Their Own For additional practice with words from the Word List, ask students to complete Worktext p. 78.

Mini-Lesson 2

Remind students that...

- the suffix -ly means "in a certain way" and the suffix -al means "relating to."
- knowing suffixes can help us learn new words.

Word List

accidental	natural
brightly	personal
directly	proudly
global	slowly
national	suddenly

Guide Practice

Use the Word List to guide practice with the suffixes -ly and -al. Write *After she sang on the TV show, Mary suddenly had global fame.* Underline *suddenly* and *global*. Read the sentence aloud with students. Ask students: What is the base word of *suddenly*? (sudden) What do you think *suddenly* means in this sentence?

("in a sudden way") The base word of *global* drops an *e* when the suffix *-al* is added. What is the base word? (globe) What does *global* mean? ("relating to the globe or world")

For the remaining words on the Word List, have students identify each base word and suffix. Then ask them to define the word and use it in a sentence.

If... students have difficulty using the words in sentences that show they understand the meaning of the word,
then... model thinking about the meaning of the word to come up with a sentence, such as *Adam did not like people going into his room or touching his personal belongings.*

On Their Own For additional practice with the words from the Word List, have students complete Worktext p. 79.

Mini-Lesson 3

Remind students that...

- the suffix -ly means "in a certain way" and the suffix -al means "relating to."
- knowing suffixes can help us learn new words.

Word List

artificially	occasional
briskly	precisely
cultural	previously
environmental	professional
experimental	roughly

Guide Practice

Use the Word List to guide practice with the suffixes -ly and -al. Write *previous* and *profession.* Read the words with students. If students do not know the meanings of the words, tell them that *previous* means "before" and that a *profession* is a type of job. Write *Jon previously was a professional football player.* Guide students as they

define the words *previously* and *professionally* using their knowledge of base words and suffixes.

Continue teaching the words from the Word List. For each word, review the meaning of the base word before asking students to define the word and use it in a sentence.

If... students cannot use the word in a sentence,
then... model a question using the base word and have students answer the question with a sentence using the word with the suffix.

On Their Own For additional practice with words from the Word List, have students complete Worktext p. 80.

Vocabulary Lesson 15
Suffixes *-ness, -ion*

Objectives:
- Learn the suffixes *-ness* and *-ion*.
- Use knowledge of suffixes to learn new words.

MATERIALS
Worktext pp. 81–83

Set the scene Introduce students to the concept of suffixes. Explain that suffixes are word parts added to the end of a word to change the meaning and that today they will learn about the suffixes *-ness* and *-ion*.

Model and teach Teach students the meanings of the suffixes *-ness* and *-ion*. Write *fairness* and *eruption*. The suffix *-ness* and *-ion* both mean "state or quality of being." When I read a word with the suffix *-ness* or *-ion* in a sentence, first I find the base word. Cover *-ness* with your hand. The base word of *fairness* is *fair*. *Fairness* means "the state of being fair." A sentence with the word *fairness* is *Mrs. Carson taught the children fairness by showing them how to share their toys*. Cover *-ion*. The base word of *eruption* is *erupt*. *Erupt* means "to begin suddenly." When a volcano erupts with lava and ash, an eruption occurs. A sentence with the word *eruption* is *A volcanic eruption can last for more than a month*. Emphasize to students that looking at word structure, or the different parts of a word, can help them figure out the meaning of unfamiliar words.

Inform students that sometimes the suffixes *-ness* and *-ion* cause spelling changes in words. Write *happiness* and *creation*. Below these words, write *happy* and *create*. Explain that sometimes adding the suffix *-ness* makes the final *y* of a base word change to an *i*. (*Silliness, dizziness,* and *weariness* are additional examples.) Then explain when the suffix *-ion* is added, base words can drop their final *e* before the suffix is added.

Mini-Lesson 1

Remind students that...
- suffixes are added at the ends of words.
- the suffix *-ness* means "state or quality of being."

Word List
darkness	kindness
dryness	loudness
coldness	shyness
gladness	sickness
goodness	softness

Guide Practice
Use the Word List to guide practice with the suffix *-ness*. Write *The loudness of the music hurt Al's ears*. Read the sentence aloud with students. Underline *loudness*.
- What base word do you see and hear in the word *loudness?* (loud)
- What does *loudness* mean? (Possible responses: "the state of being loud or noisy")

- What clues in the sentence tell you that this meaning is correct? (Possible responses: music, hurt Al's ears)

For the remaining words in the Word List, ask students to identify the base words. Then have students tell the meaning of each word and use it in a sentence.

If... students cannot supply a word meaning, **then...** review the meaning of the base word. Have students say the words *state of being* before the base word and discuss the new meaning.

On Their Own For additional practice, read the words on Worktext p. 81 with students. Ask students to complete the page.

Mini-Lesson 2

Remind students that...

- adding a suffix to the end of a word changes the word's meaning.
- the suffixes *-ness* and *-ion* mean "the state or quality of being."
- knowing the meaning of suffixes can help them learn new words.

Word List

awareness	correction
bareness	direction
boldness	eruption
brightness	gentleness
collection	greatness

Guide Practice

Use the Word List to guide practice with the suffixes *-ness* and *-ion*. Write *The teacher marked only one correction on Jamie's homework.* Read the sentence aloud with students.

- What word in sentence has the suffix *-ion*? (correction) What is the base word of the word *correction*? (correct)
- What does *correct* mean? (Possible response: "true or right")
- How does the base word *correct* relate to the word *correction*? (Possible response: A correction has the quality of being correct or right.)

Follow the same procedure with the sentence *The bareness of the room surprised Sally.* For the remainder of the Word List, have students identify the base word and suffix of each word. Then ask them to define the word and use it a sentence.

If... students have difficulty using the words in sentences that show they understand the meaning of the word,
then... model using the word in a sentence and have students try again.

On Their Own For additional practice with the words from the Word List, have students complete Worktext p. 82.

Mini-Lesson 3

Remind students that...

- adding a suffix to the end of a word changes the word's meaning.
- the suffixes *-ness* and *-ion* mean "the state or quality of being."
- sometimes adding the suffixes *-ness* or *-ion* changes the spelling of a word.

Word List

awkwardness	harshness
blindness	instruction
corruption	promotion
creation	shallowness
education	translation

Guide Practice

Use the Word List to guide practice with the suffixes *-ness* and *-ion*. Write *Chris likes his job and hopes to get a promotion.* Read the sentence aloud with students. Ask students to identify the base word and suffix of the word *promotion*. Remind them that base words that end with the suffix *-ion* sometimes drop their final *e*. Ask students to define the word and say why it makes sense in the sentence.

Continue teaching the words from the Word List. For each word, ask students to give the meaning of the base word before asking them to tell the meaning of the word with its suffix. After students supply a meaning, have them use the word in a sentence.

If... students cannot supply a meaning,
then... review the meaning of the base word.

On Their Own For additional practice with words from the Word List, have students complete Worktext p. 83.

Vocabulary Lesson 16
Suffixes *-able, -ive*

MATERIALS
Worktext pp. 84–86

Set the scene Review with students the concept of suffixes. Suffixes are word parts added to the end of a word to change the word's meaning. Today we will learn about the suffixes *-able* and *-ive*.

Model and teach Teach students the meanings of the suffixes *-able* and *-ive*. Write *laughable* and *disruptive*. The suffix *-able* means "can be." The suffix *-ive* means "likely to." When I read a word with the suffix *-able* or *-ive*, first I find the base word. Cover *-able* with your hand. The base word of *laughable* is *laugh*. *Laughable* means "can be laughed at." I read the word *disruptive* in the same way. Cover *-ive*. The base word of *disruptive* is *disrupt*. *Disrupt* means "interrupt." You can describe a sound as *disruptive*. A sentence with the words *laughable* and *disruptive* is *Sally thought that drumming on the library tables was laughable, but the noise was disruptive to other students.*

Explain to students that knowing the suffixes *-able* and *-ive* can help them understand new words as they read. When I read a word I do not know that has the suffix *-able* or *-ive*, first I read the base word. Then I put the base word into the phrase "can be" or "likely to." Then I put that meaning into the sentence to see if it makes sense. **Model** this process for students with the sentence *Stacey thought the new rules were too restrictive.* Explain to students that looking at word structure, or the different parts of a word, can help them figure out the meaning of unfamiliar words.

Mini-Lesson 1

Remind students that...
- suffixes are added to the end of a word to change the meaning of the word.
- the suffix *-able* means "can be."

Word List

acceptable	likeable
breakable	readable
comfortable	sinkable
enjoyable	traceable
learnable	washable

Guide Practice
Use the Word List to guide practice with the suffix *-able*. Write *Sophie's new bed was soft and comfortable.* Read the sentence aloud with students. Underline *comfortable*. Have students identify the suffix *-able* and the base word *comfort*. Ask them to tell the meaning of the word *comfortable*. Does this meaning make sense in the

sentence? (yes) What clues tell you that this meaning is correct? (Possible responses: The word *comfort* can describe a bed; something that is soft is usually comfortable.)

Continue using the Word List to guide practice. For the remaining words, ask students to identify the base words. Then have students tell the meaning of each word in the Word List and use it in a sentence.

If... students cannot supply a word meaning,
then... review the meaning of the base word. Have students say the words *can be* before the base word and discuss the new meaning.

On Their Own For additional practice, read the words on Worktext p. 84 with students. Ask students to complete the page.

Mini-Lesson 2

Remind students that...

- the suffix *-able* means "can be" and *-ive* means "likely or inclined to."
- knowing suffixes can help us learn new words.

Word List

active	returnable
adaptable	secretive
attractive	supportive
creative	questionable
reasonable	understandable

Guide Practice

Use the Word List to guide practice with the suffixes *-able* and *-ive*. Write *Bobcats are adaptable animals that can survive in many different places.* What is the base word of the word *adaptable*? (adapt) What does

adapt mean? (Possible response: "change in order to survive"). Ask students to define *adaptable* and say why this meaning makes sense in the sentence.

For the remaining words in the Word List, have students identify the base word and suffix of each word. Then ask them to define the word and use it a sentence. Remind students that some base words, such as *create,* drop the final *e* when the suffix *-ive* is added.

If... students cannot supply a word meaning,
then... review the meanings of the base word and the suffix. Help students choose a meaning of the suffix that works best with the base word.

On Their Own For additional practice with the words from the Word List, have students complete Worktext p. 85.

Mini-Lesson 3

Remind students that...

- the suffix *-able* means "can be" and *-ive* means "likely or inclined to."
- knowing suffixes can help us learn new words.

Word List

adjustable	inventive
avoidable	preventable
decorative	profitable
effective	recyclable
impressive	reflective

Guide Practice

Use the Word List to guide practice with the suffixes *-able* and *-ive*. Write *Elise put all the recyclable cans and bottles into the green bin.* Read the sentence aloud with students. Ask students to identify the base word and suffix of *recyclable*. Remind them that base words that end with the suffix *-able* sometimes drop the final *e*. Ask students

to define the word and say why that meaning makes sense in the sentence. Repeat the process with the word *decorative* and the sentence *Before the party, Sue placed decorative flowers and ribbons around the house.*

With students, read the rest of the words from the Word List. For each word, ask students to identify the base word and the suffix. Then have students give a meaning for each word and use it in a sentence.

If... students cannot use the word in a sentence,
then... model a sentence using the word and have them try again.

On Their Own For additional practice with words from the Word List, have students complete Worktext p. 86.

Vocabulary Lesson 17
Suffixes *-ous, -ish*

Objectives:
- Learn the suffixes *-ous* and *-ish*.
- Use the suffixes *-ous* and *-ish* to learn new words.

MATERIALS
Worktext pp. 87–89

Set the scene Review with students the concept of suffixes. A suffix is a word part added to the end of a word to change the word's meaning. Today we will learn about the suffixes *-ous* and *-ish*.

Model and teach Teach students the meanings of the suffixes *-ous* ("full of") and *-ish* ("a little bit," "sort of," or "like something"). Write *greenish* and *perilous.* When I read a word with the suffix *-ish* or *-ous* in a sentence, first I find the base word. Cover *-ish* with your hand. The base word of *greenish* is *green. Greenish* means "a little bit green." I read the word *perilous* in the same way. Cover *-ous.* The base word of *perilous* is *peril. Peril* means "danger," so a *perilous* situation is "full of danger." A sentence with the words *greenish* and *perilous* is *Robert looked into the greenish water and thought about the perilous journey ahead.*

Emphasize to students that looking at word structure, or the different parts of a word, can help them figure out the meaning of unfamiliar words. For example, knowing the suffixes *-ous* and *-ish* can help you understand new words as you read. When I read a word I do not know that has the suffix *-ish* or *-ous,* first I read the base word. Then I put the base word into the phrase "sort of" or "full of." Finally, I try that meaning in the sentence to see if it makes sense. Model this process for students with the sentence *Some plants look safe to eat but are really poisonous.*

Mini-Lesson 1

Remind students that...
- knowing suffixes can help us learn new words.
- the suffix *-ish* means "a little bit," "sort of," or "like something."

Word List
boyish	newish
childish	roundish
foolish	sickish
greenish	smallish
longish	tallish

Guide Practice
Use the Word List to guide practice. Write *Running on the ice was a foolish thing to do.* Have students identify the base word *fool* and give a meaning for the word *foolish.* How is running on ice a foolish thing to do? (Possible responses: A fool might run on ice because it is easy to slip and fall.)

Continue using the Word List to guide practice. For the remaining words, ask students to identify the base words. Then have students tell the meaning of each word and use it in a sentence.

If... students cannot supply a word meaning,
then... guide them in choosing the words *a little bit, sort of,* or *like a* before the base word and discuss the new meaning. Generally, base words that are adjectives will have the meaning "a little bit" or "sort of" while those that are nouns will have the meaning "like (something)."

On Their Own For additional practice, read the words on Worktext p. 87 with students. Ask students to complete the page.

Mini-Lesson 2

Remind students that...
- suffixes are added to the ends of words to change the meaning.
- knowing suffixes can help us learn new words.
- the suffix *-ous* means "full of."

Word List

bluish	mountainous
continuous	selfish
famous	yellowish
feverish	kittenish
joyous	youngish

Guide Practice

Use the Word List to guide practice with the suffixes *-ous* and *-ish*. Write *Many mountain climbers and hikers visit the western United States because it is mountainous.* What base word do you see and hear in the word *mountainous*? (mountain) What do you think *mountainous*

means? (Possible response: "full of mountains") Ask students to explain why this meaning makes sense in the sentence.

For the remaining words in the Word List, have students identify the base word and suffix for each word. Then ask them to define the word and use it a sentence. Remind students that some base words, such as *fame,* drop the final *e* when a suffix is added.

If... students cannot supply a sentence,

then... brainstorm with students objects or events that can be described using words from the Word List. For example, a wedding can be "full of joy," so a sentence with the word *joyous* is *The wedding photos helped us remember the joyous day.*

On Their Own For additional practice with the words from the Word List, have students complete Worktext p. 88.

Mini-Lesson 3

Remind students that...
- knowing suffixes helps them learn new words when they read.
- sometimes base words drop the final e when a suffix is added.

Word List

cavernous	sheepish
marvelous	stylish
virtuous	purplish
courageous	nightmarish
hazardous	humorous

Guide Practice

Use the Word List to guide practice with the suffixes *-ish* and *-ous*. Write *Maria looked very stylish with her new haircut and sunglasses.* Ask students to identify the base word and suffix of *stylish.* Then have students define the word and say why that meaning makes sense in the

sentence. Follow the same procedure with *virtuous* and the sentence *Mark seemed like a virtuous person who never told lies.*

Read the rest of the words from the Word List. For each word, ask students to identify the base word and the suffix. Then have them give a meaning for the word and use it in a sentence.

If... students cannot supply a word meaning,

then... review the meanings of the base word and of the suffix. Invite students to look up difficult base words, such as *marvel* and *cavern,* in a dictionary.

On Their Own For additional practice with words from the Word List, have students complete Worktext p. 89.

Vocabulary Lesson 18
Synonyms

Objectives:
- Learn synonyms.
- Learn how synonyms can be clues to meaning in sentences.

MATERIALS
Worktext pp. 90–92

Set the scene
Review with students the concept of synonyms. Some words mean the same or almost the same thing. These words are called *synonyms.* When you talk or write, you can choose between synonyms to talk about the same idea.

Model and teach
Teach students how to identify synonyms. Write *alone.* Below it write *gorgeous, solitary,* and *daring.* The word *alone* has a synonym in this Word List. Read the words aloud. To find the synonym, I think of what I know about each word. Then I decide which words mean the same or almost the same thing. I know that *alone* means "away from other people." *Gorgeous* means "pretty." *Gorgeous* is not a synonym for *alone.* Cross out *gorgeous.* *Daring* means "brave." Someone who is *solitary* is by him- or herself. *Solitary* and *alone* are synonyms. Another synonym of *alone* is *isolated.*

Model for students how to use synonyms to determine the meaning of an unfamiliar word in a sentence. When I read a word I do not know in a sentence, I look for a synonym nearby. Write *This year Rick will ascend a mountain in Europe. He will climb a mountain in South America, too.* I am going to look for a synonym to help me figure out the meaning of *ascend.* Underline *climb.* I know that "climb" means "to go up." Circle the word *too.* The word *too* means "also" and tells me that *climb* and *ascend* might be synonyms. To check, I say the sentence with the word *climb* instead of *ascend* to see if the sentence has the same meaning: *This year Rick will climb a mountain in Europe. He will climb a mountain in South America, too.* Explain to students that they can use a thesaurus to find synonyms for words.

Mini-Lesson 1

Remind students that...
- some words have the same or nearly the same meaning.
- words can have more than one synonym.

Word List

big	little
drag	pull
fast	quick
huge	small
large	tug

Guide Practice
Use the Word List to guide practice with synonyms. Say the sentence *The strap on Sara's bag broke, so she had to drag the bag across the ground.* Write *drag, small, pull, fast, tug,* and *little.* Read the words aloud.

- What does *drag* mean? (Possible response: "hold onto something and move it across a surface")
- Which of these words is a synonym for *drag*? (pull)
- If you substitute the word *pull* for the word *drag* in the sentence, does the sentence make sense? (yes)
- What is another synonym of *pull* in the list? (tug)

Ask students to identify other words in the list that are synonyms (*small* and *little*). Then ask them to provide another synonym for *little* and to create a sentence that includes that word.

If... students have difficulty understanding that some words can have many synonyms,

then... ask them to think of all the words to describe something in the room. Discuss which words are synonyms.

On Their Own For additional practice, ask students to complete Worktext p. 90.

Mini-Lesson 2

Remind students that…
- synonyms have the same or nearly the same meaning.
- looking for synonyms in sentences can help us figure out unfamiliar words.

Word List

choose	select
clever	shout
journey	smart
mystery	voyage
puzzle	yell

Guide Practice
Use the Word List to guide practice with synonyms. Write *I heard Rose yell, and I heard Kim shout too.* Underline *yell.* Which word in this sentence means the same thing as *yell*? **(shout)** What clue word helped you figure out the synonym? **(too)** What is another synonym

for *yell* and *shout*? (Possible responses: holler, scream, cry out)

Write the remaining words from the Word List and guide students as they pair the synonyms: *clever/smart, voyage/journey, mystery/puzzle,* and *choose/select.* For each pair, have students supply an example sentence. Then ask them to replace one synonym with the other in each sentence.

If… students have difficulty understanding synonyms, **then…** ask them more questions about the words and draw attention to the similarities in meaning between the word pairs.

On Their Own For additional practice with the words from the Word List, have students complete Worktext p. 91.

Mini-Lesson 3

Remind students that…
- synonyms have the same or nearly the same meaning.
- looking for synonyms in sentences can help us learn new words.

Word List

bashful	piece
observe	fragment
notice	timid
mistake	display
error	exhibit

Guide Practice
Use the Word List to guide practice with synonyms. Write *Jim is a shy, timid person. You can tell he is bashful because he speaks quietly and does not look people in the eyes.* Underline *bashful.* From these sentences, what do you think *bashful* means? (Possible responses: shy, quiet, not sociable) Which words in the sentences are

synonyms for *bashful*? (*shy* and *timid*) Replace the word *bashful* with *shy* in the sentence. Does the sentence have the same meaning? (yes)

Follow the same procedure with the sentence *The first baseman made three errors, and the pitcher made mistakes as well.* Guide students as they identify *errors* and *mistakes* as synonyms. Point out that, like the word *too,* the phrase *as well* can be a clue that two words mean the same thing.

If… students have difficulty replacing the synonyms, **then…** remind them to ask themselves if the word makes sense in the sentence.

On Their Own For additional practice with words from the Word List, have students complete Worktext p. 92.

Vocabulary Lesson 19
Unfamiliar Words

Objectives:
- Learn that writers sometimes explain or define a word within a sentence or paragraph.
- Use context to determine the meanings of unfamiliar words.

MATERIALS

Worktext pp. 93–95

Set the scene
Review with students the concept of unfamiliar words. When you come across a word that you do not know, you can often figure out what the word means by looking at the words and sentences around the word. You can also look up an unfamiliar word in a dictionary or glossary.

Model and teach
Teach students how to use context to determine the meaning of an unfamiliar word. Write *Today for the first time I ate a pomegranate, a red fruit with about a million seeds.* Read the sentence aloud and underline *pomegranate.* If I do not know the meaning of *pomegranate* in this sentence, I can look for clues to figure out its meaning. Sometimes an author will define a word or explain its meaning. In this sentence, the author tells me that a pomegranate is "a red fruit with about a million seeds." The words *or, that is, which means,* or a comma can be clues that a definition is included in the sentence.

Write *At the fruit stand, we bought apples, pomegranates, and blueberries.* In this sentence, the author does not define *pomegranate.* However, there are other clues to the word's meaning. I know that the author bought a pomegranate at a fruit stand. I also know that the author lists the word with *apples* and *blueberries.* With this information, I can guess that a pomegranate is a kind of fruit. This meaning makes sense in the sentence. To learn more about pomegranates, I can look up the word in a dictionary.

Mini-Lesson 1

Remind students that...
- sometimes a word is defined or explained within a sentence.
- the words *or, that is, which means,* or a comma can signal a meaning in a sentence.

Word List

cottage	parka
freeway	puma
mallard	rye
mound	skiff
pansy	snout

Guide Practice
Use the Word List to guide practice with unfamiliar words. Write *At the zoo we saw a puma, or big wild cat.* Read the sentence aloud. Let's use the words around the word *puma* to figure out the word's meaning.

- What clue word tells you that the author included a meaning in this sentence? **(or)** Circle *or.* What meaning did the author give? **(big wild cat)**
- How does this meaning make sense with the rest of the sentence? **(Possible response: It makes sense because you might see a big wild cat at a zoo.)**

Follow the same procedure with the sentence *Cal wore his parka–that is, a heavy coat–to play in the snow.*

If... children have difficulty understanding how the phrases can help them,

then... read the sentences without those words. Then read the complete sentence again and discuss the clues that the words give to the reader.

On Their Own For additional practice, ask students to complete Worktext p. 93.

Mini-Lesson 2

Remind students that…
- sometimes you can use the words around an unfamiliar word to figure out its meaning.
- if a meaning is not given, you can predict a meaning for the word using other clues.

Word List

banjo	produce
banquet	roast
modest	tether
mumps	toboggan
pasture	weep

Guide Practice
Use the Word List to guide practice with unfamiliar words. Write *Jeff got on his toboggan and slid down the snowy hill.* Read the sentence and underline the word *toboggan.* What does the sentence tell you about the word *toboggan*? (Possible responses: It is something

you get on; you use it to slide down snowy hills.) From the clues in the sentence, predict what *toboggan* means. How would you define *toboggan*? (Possible response: a sled) Insert your prediction in the sentence. Does the sentence make sense with this meaning of the word? (yes)

Follow the same procedure with the sentence *Emily saw a hundred cows standing or eating grass in the pasture.* Have students predict a meaning for the word *pasture* and try that meaning in the sentence.

If… students have difficulty predicting a meaning for an unfamiliar word,
then… identify one clue that supports the correct meaning, and ask students to identify additional clues.

On Their Own For additional practice with the words from the Word List, have students complete Worktext p. 94.

Mini-Lesson 3

Remind students that…
- sometimes you can use the words around an unfamiliar word to figure out its meaning.
- sometimes clues can be found in surrounding sentences.

Word List

allegiance	parasol
clamor	procession
competent	pueblo
consistent	rehearse
infantry	symmetry

Guide Practice
Use the Word List to guide practice with unfamiliar words. Write *Kristy held a parasol above her head. Sam asked, "Why do you have that? It's not raining!" Kristy replied that she did not want the sun to touch her face.* Underline *parasol.* Guide students as they use context to predict a

meaning for the word *parasol.* Ask them to identify clues within all three sentences. Then ask them to insert the meaning they determine into the first sentence.

Repeat this procedure with the word *rehearse* and these sentences: *To prepare for the big show, Amanda and Kim practiced twice a day. Kim thought it was silly to rehearse so often. Amanda promised her all the time and effort would be worth it.*

If… students have difficulty identifying clues in surrounding sentences,
then… read only the sentence that contains the unfamiliar word before adding the other sentences. Ask what helpful information the other sentences provide.

On Their Own For additional practice, have students complete Worktext p. 95.

Vocabulary Lesson 20
Word Endings *-s, -es*

Objectives:
- Learn about the word endings *-s* and *-es*.
- Use the *-s* or *-es* word endings to learn new words.

MATERIALS
Worktext pp. 96–98

Set the scene
Review with students the concept of word endings. Today we are going to talk about the word endings *-s* and *-es*. When these endings are added to nouns, they make the nouns mean "more than one," as in *toys*. When these endings are added to verbs, they describe actions happening now or repeatedly, as in *Laura walks to school every day.*

Model and teach
Teach students how to recognize plurals with the word endings *-s* or *-es*. To make most nouns plural, *-s* is added to the end of the word. Write *claws*. What is the base word of *claws*? (claw) What does *claws* mean? ("more than one claw")

Write *dishes, lunches, bosses, waltzes,* and *taxes,* and circle the *-es* ending in each word. What does the *-es* ending tell you about all of these words? (They're plural.) The *-es* ending is used when the base word ends with *s, sh, ch, x,* or *z*. Help students recognize word endings that cause spelling changes in the base word such as in the word *city*.

When you see the endings *-s* and *-es* on verbs, or action words, they describe actions happening in the present or that happen repeatedly. Write *Sam plays.* Underline the verb and circle the ending. The *-s* in *plays* tells you that Sam is playing right now. Write *Sam studies every day.* This tells you that Sam studies repeatedly. Emphasize to students that looking at word structure, or the different parts of a word, can help them figure out the meaning of unfamiliar words.

Mini-Lesson 1

Remind students that...
- the word endings *-s* and *-es* can be added to nouns and verbs.
- when the word endings *-s* and *-es* are added to nouns, they make the nouns mean "more than one," as in *toys*.
- when the word endings *-s* and *-es* are added to verbs, they describe actions happening now or repeatedly.

Word List

baskets	grasses
boxes	lunches
bunnies	monkeys
falls	stops
flies	washes

Guide Practice
Use the Word List to guide practice with the word endings *-s* and *-es*. Write the nouns *baskets, bunnies,* and *grasses* in one column. Write the verbs *stops, washes,* and *flies* in another.

- Point to the word *baskets*. What word ending do you see? (*-s*) How does this word ending change the meaning of the word *basket*? (Possible response: It makes it mean more than one basket.)
- Point to *bunnies*. What is the base word? (bunny)
- What spelling change was made to this word to make it plural? (The *y* was changed to an *i* before adding *-es*.)
- Point to *flies*. What is the base word? (fly)
- What are some meanings of *fly*? (Possible responses: "to travel in the air," "a bug with wings")
- Think about *fly* as an action and think of the word ending *-es*. What does the word ending *-es* tell you about the meaning of the word? (It tells you that the action is happening right now.)

If... students have difficulty recognizing plurals,
then... remind them of the spelling rules and provide additional examples.

On Their Own For additional practice, ask students to complete Worktext p. 96.

Mini-Lesson 2

Remind students that...

- the word endings -s and -es can be added to nouns and verbs.
- when the word endings -s and -es are added to nouns, they make the nouns mean "more than one," as in *essays*.
- when the word endings -s and -es are added to verbs, they describe actions happening now or repeatedly.

Word List

cameras	presses
finishes	quits
glasses	reaches
libraries	relaxes
peaches	strawberries

Guide Practice

Use the Word List to guide practice with the word endings -s and -es. Write *At the store, Mom bought peaches, two boxes of strawberries, and apples.* How many plural words are in the sentence? (four) What are they? (peaches, boxes, strawberries, and apples) Did the mother buy one of each? How do you know? (No, the mom bought more than one of each. I know because of the word endings -es and -s.)

Continue using the Word List to teach word endings. Write the verbs *finish, reach, relax, press,* and *quit.* Have students tell you what -s or -es tell them about the verbs, and have students use the words in sentences.

If... students have difficulty recognizing the -es ending, **then...** slowly say words ending in *ch, sh, ss, x,* and *z* that take -es, such as *peaches* and *boxes.* Have students listen for the *e* sound at the end of the word.

On Their Own For additional practice, have students complete Worktext p. 97.

Mini-Lesson 3

Remind students that...

- the word endings -s and -es can be added to nouns and verbs.
- when the word endings -s and -es are added to nouns, they make the nouns mean "more than one," as in *toys*.
- when the word endings -s and -es are added to verbs, they describe actions happening now or repeatedly.

Word List

approaches	horizons
diminishes	multiplies
galaxies	myths
graduates	recipes
harnesses	waltzes

Guide Practice

Use the Word List to guide practice with the word endings -s and -es. Write *Paul graduates today, and he has to give a speech. He approaches the microphone, and his nervousness multiplies.* Then read the sentences aloud. What three words are actions that are happening now? (graduates, approaches, multiplies) Underline the words and ask students to circle the word endings. What do the word endings tell you about the verbs? (They are happening right now.) Students may need to be reminded that, when a base word ends with a consonant and *y*, they need to change the *y* to an *i* before adding -es.

Write the remaining words from the Word List. Then have students use the words in sentences.

If... students have difficulty understanding the meaning of the words,
then... focus on the meaning of the base words first.

On Their Own For additional practice with words from the Word List, have students complete Worktext p. 98.

Vocabulary Lesson 21
Word Endings *-ed, -ing*

Objectives:
- Learn about the word endings *-ed* and *-ing*.
- Use and recognize verbs ending in *-ed* and *-ing*.

MATERIALS

Worktext pp. 99–101

Set the scene

Introduce students to the concept of word endings. Today we are going to talk about the word endings *-ed* and *-ing*. These endings are added to verbs to change the tense of verbs. Verbs ending in *-ing* describe continuous actions, or actions that do not start and then stop. The ending *-ed* describes an action that happened in the past.

Model and teach

Teach students about the endings *-ed* and *-ing*. Write *walking, colliding,* and *canoeing* and read them aloud. What are the base words of these words? (walk, collide, canoe) Review the meaning of each word. We know that *walk* is an action that means "to move with one's feet." Walk across the room. Right now I am *walking* across the room. The word *walking* has the ending *-ing*. It describes an action that is happening now. Stop at the other end of the room. I just *walked* across the room. The word *walked* has the ending *-ed*. It describes an action that happened in the past. I can also say *I was walking across the room.* In this sentence, the word *walking* describes a continuous action that happened in the past.

Point out to students common spelling changes that occur when adding *-ed* and *-ing*. Point to *collide.* The word *collide* means "crash into." Notice that *collide* ends with an *e*, and that the letter before *e* is the consonant *d*. When I add the word ending *-ing* to *collide*, it drops the final *e*. Write *colliding*. Point to *canoe.* Canoe has a vowel before its final *e*, so the spelling does not change when I add *-ing*. Write *canoeing*. Emphasize to students that looking at word structure, or the different parts of a word, can help them figure out the meaning of unfamiliar words.

Mini-Lesson 1

Remind students that...
- the word endings *-ed* and *-ing* change the tense of verbs.
- recognizing *-ed* and *-ing* endings can help them learn new words.

Word List

closed	finishing
closing	jumped
cooked	jumping
cooking	snowed
finished	snowing

Guide Practice

Use the Word List to guide practice with the word endings *-ed* and *-ing*. Write the words *closed, closing, finished,* and *finishing*. Invite students to circle the *-ed* or *-ing* ending in each word. Listen to these sentences: *The store closed. The store is closing.* How do the word endings *-ed* and *-ing* make the sentences mean different things? (Possible responses: In the first sentence, the store is not open. In the second sentence, the store is still open, but it is about to close.) Remind students that the word *close* drops the final *e* when a word ending is added.

Repeat with the sentences *Ana finished her homework. Ana is finishing her homework.*

If... students have difficulty understanding the difference between *-ed* and *-ing*,
then... pantomime or act out actions, when possible. Ask students *What am I doing now? What did I just do?*

On Their Own For additional practice with words from the Word List, ask students to complete Worktext p. 99.

Mini-Lesson 2

Remind students that…

- the word endings -*ed* and -*ing* change the tense of verbs.
- recognizing -*ed* and -*ing* endings can help them learn new words.

Word List

chased	counting
chasing	flashed
complained	flashing
complaining	smiled
counted	smiling

Guide Practice

Use the Word List to guide practice with the word endings -*ed* and -*ing*. Remind students that the -*ing* ending can be used to talk about a continuous action that happened in the past.

Write *flashed*. What is the base word? (flash) The word *flash* means "shine suddenly." What does the ending -*ed* tell you about when this action happens? (It tells that it happened in the past.)

Listen to these sentences: The lightning flashed. The lightning is flashing outside my window. Which sentence talks about something that is happening right now? (the second sentence) How do you know? (the word ending –*ing*)

Follow the same procedure with the words *chasing* and *chased* and the sentences *The policeman is chasing the thief. The policeman chased the thief.*

If… students have difficulty understanding word endings,
then… ask them to tell a story about something from the past. Point out -*ed* and -*ing* words they use.

On Their Own For additional practice, have students complete Worktext p. 100.

Mini-Lesson 3

Remind students that…

- the word endings -*ed* and -*ing* change the tense of verbs.
- recognizing -*ed* and -*ing* endings can help them learn new words.

Word List

canceled	guiding
canceling	recovered
challenged	recovering
challenging	surrounded
guided	surrounding

Guide Practice

Use the Word List to guide practice with the word endings -*ed* and -*ing*. Write *Fans surrounded the movie star*. Which word in this sentence has the word ending -*ed* or -*ing*? (surrounded) What is the base word? (surround) What does *surround* mean? (Possible response: circle)

Now add -*ing* to *surround*. What is a sentence with this word? (Possible response: The long line is surrounding the building.) Inform students that sometimes verbs that end in -*ing* act as adjectives, as in the phrases "the surrounding areas" and "the laughing girl."

Follow the same procedure with the remaining words from the Word List. For each word, ask students to add one or both word endings and to use the word in a sentence.

If… students have difficulty understanding how a verb can act as an adjective,
then… provide examples from the Word List. In the sentence *The recovering athlete saw his trainer five times a week,* the word *recovering* describes the athlete.

On Their Own For additional practice, have students complete Worktext p. 101.

Vocabulary Lesson 22
Homographs

Objectives:
- Learn about homographs.
- Use context to determine correct meanings and pronunciations of homographs.

MATERIALS

Worktext pp. 102–104

Set the scene Introduce students to the concept of homographs. Homographs are words that have the same spelling but different meanings. Some homographs, such as *dove* (rhyming with *love*) and *dove* (rhyming with *cove*), sound different from one another.

Model and teach Give students an example of homographs. Write *Who will lead the parade?* Read the sentence aloud. Underline *lead*. In this sentence, the word *lead* rhymes with *bead*. *Lead* means "to go first." Write *I need to put more lead in my pencil.* This sentence also has a word spelled *l, e, a, d.* In this sentence, the word *lead* rhymes with *red*. *Lead* is the dark material inside a pencil. The words *lead* (rhyming with bead) and *lead* (rhyming with red) are homographs. They are spelled exactly the same, but they sound different and have different meanings.

Model for students how to use context clues to determine the meaning of a homograph in a sentence. Write *Please close the door after you come in.* Underline *close*. There are two ways to say the word spelled *c, l, o, s, e*. The word *close* rhymes with *dose* and is an adjective that means "near." The word *close* rhymes with *nose* and is a verb that means "shut." To figure out the correct meaning and pronunciation, I will substitute the meanings I know for *c, l, o, s, e* into the sentence. *Please near the door after you come in* does not make sense. *Please shut the door after you come in* does make sense. In this sentence, *close* rhymes with *nose*. Explain to students that they used context clues to help them determine which homograph to use in the sentence.

Remind students that...
- homographs look the same but have different meanings.
- some homographs have different pronunciations.

Word List

bow	live
close	tap
date	tear
fan	wake
jam	wind

Guide Practice

Use the Word List to guide practice with homographs. Write *The strong wind shook the house.* Read the sentence aloud and underline the word *wind*. In this sentence, *wind* rhymes with *grinned* and means "moving air." Is there another word that is spelled *w, i, n, d*? (yes) How do you say this word? (*wind* rhymes with *kind*)

When *wind* rhymes with *kind*, what does the word mean? (Possible response: "curve") What is a sentence that uses the word *wind*? (Possible response: The roads wind through the mountains.)

Follow this procedure with the homograph *jam* and the sentence *Erin put butter and jam on her toast.* Remind students that all homographs have different meanings, but not all homographs have different pronunciations.

If... students have difficulty distinguishing the pronunciation for the homographs,
then... insert the incorrect pronunciation of a homograph into a sentence. Tell students to listen carefully and think about which pronunciation sounds right.

On Their Own For additional practice with homographs, ask students to complete Worktext p. 102.

Mini-Lesson 2

Remind students that...
- homographs look the same but have different meanings.
- some homographs have different pronunciations.

Word List

bass	lead
desert	mean
does	minute
dove	present
hide	wound

Guide Practice

Use the Word List to guide practice with homographs. Write *dove*. What two words are spelled *d, o, v, e*? (*Dove* rhymes with *love*; *dove* rhymes with *cove*.) What does *dove* (rhymes with *cove*) mean? (**past tense of** *dive*) What does *dove* (rhymes with *love*) mean? (**"a white bird"**) Write *The diver took a deep breath and _____ into the*

water. Julie found a feather from a white _____. Read the sentences. Pause or say "blank" in place of the blanks. Discuss with students which meaning and pronunciation fits in each sentence. Then invite students to say the sentences aloud with the correct pronunciation of *dove.*

Follow the same procedure with the homograph *mean* and the following sentences: *Tom's big brother is mean and always teases Tom. Do you understand what I mean?*

If... students have difficulty choosing a meaning of a homograph,
then... review the meanings of the homographs for students and ask them to use each word in a sentence.

On Their Own For additional practice, have students complete Worktext p. 103.

Mini-Lesson 3

Remind students that...
- homographs look the same but have different meanings.
- some homographs have different pronunciations.

Word List

address	buffet
content	conflict
contract	entrance
crooked	lumber
invalid	loaf

Guide Practice

Use the Word List to guide practice with homographs. Write *Every time you move, a muscle will expand and then contract.* Underline *contract.*
- What does *contract* mean in this sentence? (Possible response: "get smaller")

- What other word has this spelling, and what does that word mean? (Possible response: "a legal document")
- What is a sentence with this word? (Possible response: The plumber signed a contract stating the work would be finished in two weeks.) Listen to the words: *contract* from the first sentence and *contract* from the second. The words sound slightly different. *Contract* and *contract* are homographs.

Follow the same procedure with the homograph *address* and the following sentences: *When the Smiths move to Virginia, they will have a new address. The governor will give an address from the state capital today.*

If... students do not know the meanings of a homograph,
then... guide students as they look up the homograph in a dictionary and read each given definition.

On Their Own For additional practice, have students complete Worktext p. 104.

Dictionary, Glossary, and Thesaurus

Objectives:
- Understand how to use a dictionary, glossary, and thesaurus to look up words.
- Learn the different parts of dictionary, glossary, and thesaurus entries.

MATERIALS

Worktext pp. 105–107

Set the scene Review with students the concept of dictionaries, glossaries, and thesauruses. When you read a word that you do not know, you can look up its meaning in a dictionary or glossary. A glossary comes at the end of a book and includes words from the book. You can also use a thesaurus to find words that have a similar meaning or an opposite meaning.

Model and teach Model how to use a dictionary for students. Write *There was dissent among the members of the club.* Read the sentence aloud. Underline *dissent*. This sentence does not tell me much about the word *dissent*. I will look up the word to figure out its meaning. If possible, look up the word *dissent* and show students the actual entry. Dictionaries, glossaries, and thesauruses list words in alphabetical, or *ABC* order. To find *dissent,* I go to the "d" section of the dictionary.

Talk through with students the parts of a dictionary entry. Write *dis•sent.* In a dictionary, the word I look up is called the *entry word.* Entry words are listed in bold. The dot in between *dis* and *sent* shows the syllables, or how many beats are in the word. Say and clap *dis, sent. Dissent* has two syllables. The dictionary lists two definitions for *dissent.* When a dictionary gives more than one meaning for a word, I see which meaning makes the most sense in the sentence. Read the definitions of dissent: *1. to differ in opinion; disagree* and *2. difference of opinion; disagreement.* Explain how the second definition makes the most sense in the sentence. Then inform students that many dictionaries and glossaries include other features, such as example sentences and pronunciation.

Remind students that...
- dictionaries and glossaries list words and meanings.
- dictionaries and glossaries are organized in *ABC* order.

Word List

cartoon	shelter
flood	soil
insect	timber
parent	wheat
pebble	width

Guide Practice

Use the Word List to guide practice with dictionaries. Write the words *width, cartoon, timber,* and *soil.* Look at the first letters of these words. Which word would be listed first in a dictionary? (cartoon) Look up *cartoon* in a children's or junior dictionary. Write *car•toon.* Ask students how many beats the word has. If possible, have students read the definition or definitions. After hearing

the word's meaning, ask students to use *cartoon* in a sentence.

Follow the same procedure with the remaining words. As students determine which words come next in a dictionary, rewrite the words in alphabetical order.

If... students have difficulty placing words in *ABC* order, **then...** write the alphabet, and draw lines between the first letters of words and the letter in the alphabet.

On Their Own For additional practice putting words in *ABC* order, ask students to complete Worktext p. 105.

Mini-Lesson 2

Remind students that…

- dictionaries, glossaries, and thesauruses give information about words.
- dictionary entries give information about how to use a word in a sentence.

Word List

barrier	sculpture
magnify	telegraph
margin	transportation
population	villain
publish	weight

Guide Practice

Use the Word List to guide practice with dictionaries. Explain that they will look up entry words in a dictionary. Tell them that they will read the sentences and phrases that show how to use the word. Then write *sculpture*.

- Let's look up the word *sculpture.* It has a few definitions. What is the first definition? (Possible response: "the art of carving or modeling figures") What is another definition of *sculpture*? (Possible response: "a figure made in this way")
- How is the word used in a phrase or sentence in the dictionary? (Possible response: *There are many famous sculptures in the museum.*)

Follow the same procedure with additional words from the Word List. After students read the sentences or phrases in the dictionary entry, ask them to use the words in a sentence of their own.

If… students have difficulty locating example sentences or phrases in a dictionary,
then… tell students that example sentences are often in italic, or slanted, type.

On Their Own For additional practice, have students complete Worktext p. 106.

Mini-Lesson 3

Remind students that…

- dictionaries list words and their meanings.
- some dictionaries give information about how to say and use a word.

Word List

audience	immigrate
ballad	pamphlet
biography	perpetual
evaporate	rotation
herbivore	summary

Guide Practice

Use the Word List to guide practice with dictionaries. Write *Over time, the water will evaporate.* Underline *evaporate*. Ask students to look up *evaporate* in a dictionary. Point to the pronunciation key in a sample dictionary. Use the pronunciation key and the letters and symbols in parentheses. How do you say this word?

Guide students as they sound out the symbols in the pronunciation key. The letter before the definition gives the part of speech. What letter do you see? (*v*) That's right, the *v* means that *evaporate* is a verb, or action word.

Follow the same procedure with additional words from the Word List. As appropriate, explain the abbreviations for different parts of speech in dictionary entries.

If… students have difficulty reading the pronunciation key,
then… make sure they know how to pronounce the example words given for each symbol. Read through the pronunciation key, so students are certain of the sounds the symbols represent.

On Their Own For additional practice, have students complete Worktext p. 107.

Vocabulary Lesson 24
Context Clues

MATERIALS
Worktext pp. 108–110

Set the scene

Review with students the concept of context clues. When you read, you will often come across a word that you do not know. Sometimes you can figure out the word's meaning by paying attention to context, or nearby words and sentences. Today we are going to learn how examples, synonyms, and antonyms act as context clues.

Model and teach

Explain to students that examples in sentences can give clues about the definition of a word. Tell students to look for clue words that signal examples (*such as, like, including*). Write and read aloud: *The library has many periodicals, such as newspapers, magazines,* and *journals.* Underline *periodicals.* What clue words do you see? (such as) What examples does it introduce? (newspapers, magazines, journals) What do these examples tell you about the definition of *periodical*? (It's a type of publication that is published often.)

Explain to students that synonyms are words that have similar meanings, such as *scream* and *shout.* The clue word *too* signals synonyms. Write and read aloud: *We told an abundant number of toys at the garage sale, and our neighbors sold a great number too.* Underline *abundant.* What clue word do you see? (too) What does it tell you about *great*? (that it's a synonym of *abundant*) How does this synonym help you figure out the definition of *abundant*? (*Possible response:* It tells me that *abundant* means "great" or "plentiful.")

Repeat the process with antonyms. Tell students that antonyms are words that mean the opposite, such as *whisper* and *yell.* The clue word *but* signals antonyms.

Remind students that...
- they can use surrounding words and sentences to figure out unfamiliar words.
- examples are a type of context clue.
- clue words that signal examples are *such as, like,* and *including.*

Word List

boundary	seasoning
equipment	supplies
furniture	technology
instruments	transportation
linens	utensils

Guide Practice
Use the Word List to guide practice with context clues. Focus on examples as a type of context clue. Tell students to look for clue words that signal examples (*such as, like, including*).

Write *The meat had several seasonings I didn't like, such as oregano and pepper.*
- What clue words are in this sentence? (such as)
- What examples do they introduce? (oregano, pepper)
- Based on the examples, what do you think the meaning of *seasoning* is? (a type of spice)

Follow the same procedure with the remaining words in the Word List.

If... students have difficulty identifying examples, **then...** practice looking for the clue words *such as, like,* and *including.*

On Their Own For additional practice, ask students to complete Worktext p. 108.

Mini-Lesson 2

Remind students that…

- they can use surrounding words and sentences to figure out unfamiliar words.
- synonyms and antonyms are types of context clues.
- the clue word *too* signals synonyms are *too* and the clue word *but* signals antonyms.

Word List

astounded	radiant
cowardly	revolves
crisis	rugged
displeased	terrible
humid	transmits

Guide Practice

Use the Word List to guide practice with context clues. Focus on synonyms and antonyms as types of context clues. Explain to students that synonyms are words that have similar meanings, such as *cold* and *chilly*. Antonyms are words with opposite meanings, such as *cold* and *hot*. Tell students to look for the clue word *too,* which signals synonyms, or the clue word *but,* which signals antonyms.

Write *The weather was terrible today, and tomorrow it will be awful too.*

- What clue word do you see in this sentence? (too)
- What does it tell you? (that *awful* is a synonym of *terrible*)
- Based on the examples, what do you think the meaning of *terrible* is? ("very bad")

Follow the same procedure with the remaining words in the Word List.

If… students have difficulty distinguishing between antonyms and synonyms,

then… tell them to first identify the clue words *too* or *but.*

On Their Own For additional practice, have students complete Worktext p. 109.

Mini-Lesson 3

Remind students that…

- they can use surrounding words and sentences to figure out unfamiliar words.
- examples, synonyms, and antonyms are types of context clues.

Word List

accessories	grateful
ancient	persistent
aviator	perspective
confident	reject
currency	robust

Guide Practice

Remind students that synonyms are words with similar meanings (*huge, giant*), and antonyms are words with opposite meanings (*huge, small*). Tell students that the clue word *too* signals synonyms, the clue word *but* signals antonyms, and the clue words *such as, including,* and *like* all signal examples.

Write *Tim was grateful for Maria's help, and Maria was thankful too for the gift he gave her.*

- What clue word do you see in this sentence? (too)
- What does it tell you? (that *thankful* is a synonym of *grateful*)
- Based on the examples, what do you think the meaning of *grateful* is? ("feeling or showing appreciation")

Follow the same procedure with the remaining words in the Word List.

If… students have difficulty distinguishing between antonyms, synonyms, and examples,

then… tell them to first identify the clue words and spend time connecting the clue words to the type of context clue.

On Their Own For additional practice, have students complete Worktext p. 110.

Vocabulary Lesson 25
Word Structure

Objectives:
- Understand and identify word parts, including base words, word endings, small words within compound words, prefixes, and suffixes.
- Use knowledge of word parts to decode new words.

MATERIALS
Worktext pp. 111–113

Set the scene Review with students the concept of word structure. When you read a new word, it is helpful to look at the different parts of the word. Today we will learn how to read words that have more than one part.

Model and teach Model reading a word with a word ending. Write *throwing*. The word *throwing* has the word ending *-ing*. To read words with word endings, first I read the base word. Cover *-ing*. The base word of *throwing* is the verb *throw*. Then I read the whole word together: *throw, ing, throwing*. A sentence with this word is *I am throwing the ball to you.*

Explain to students how to use word parts to figure out the meaning of a word. Write *moveable*. The suffix *-able* means "can be." To figure out the meaning of the word *moveable*, I think about the meaning of the base word and the meaning of the suffix together. Cover *-able*. The base word of *moveable* is *move*. *Moveable* means "can be moved."

Repeat the process with a word with more than two word parts. Some words have more than one added word part. Write *adoringly*. This word has the suffix *-ly*. Cover *-ly*. However, *adoring* is not a base word. This word can still be broken down. Cover *-ing*. To figure out the base word *adore*, I have to remember that some words lose their final *e* when you add a word ending. *Adoringly* means "in an adoring way."

Remind students that instead of a base word and an added word part, compound words like *baseball* and *firefly* can be broken into two small words.

Remind students that...
- word parts are base words, word endings, small words within compound words, prefixes, and suffixes.
- words can have more than one word part.
- they can use word parts to determine a word's meaning.

Word List

airplane	precook
bedroom	promised
darkish	smallest
drinkable	unhappy
fairly	yelling

Guide Practice
Use the Word List to guide practice with word structure. Write *The tea was so hot it was not drinkable.* Read the sentence with students. Point to the word *drinkable*. The word *drinkable* has the suffix *-able*. The suffix *-able* means "can be." What base word do you see and hear in the word *drinkable*? (drink) What do you think *drinkable* means? (Possible response: you can drink it) Does this meaning make sense in the sentence? (yes) Inform students that adding the prefix *un-* to *drinkable* creates the word *undrinkable,* which means "not drinkable."

For the remaining words on the Word List, ask students to identify the base words and added word parts. Guide students as they use word parts to determine the words' meanings. Then ask them to use each word in a sentence.

If... students have difficulty identifying word parts, **then...** cover part of the word with your hand as a hint.

On Their Own For additional practice with word structure, ask students to complete Worktext p. 111.

Remind students that...

• word parts are base words, word endings, small words within compound words, prefixes, and suffixes.

• words can have more than one word part.

• they can use word parts to determine the meaning of a word.

Word List

arguable	misdirect
blended	postcard
delightful	smoothly
driveway	unaware
greatness	uncommon

Guide Practice

Use the Word List to guide practice with word structure. Write *It is uncommon to see pandas in the wild.* Which word in this sentence can be broken into word parts? (uncommon) What prefix or suffix do you see in the

word *uncommon*? (*un-*) The prefix *un-* means "not." How would you define *uncommon*? ("not common") Does this meaning make sense in the sentence? (yes) Write *uncommonly.* How is this word alike and different from the word *uncommon*? (Possible response: Both words have *common* as a base word; *uncommonly* has the added suffix *-ly.*) Inform students that *uncommonly* means "in an uncommon way."

Ask students to identify the word parts of the remaining words on the Word List. Help students define each word. Then ask them to use the words in sentences.

If... students have difficulty supplying sentences, **then...** model a sentence, and ask them to try again.

On Their Own For additional practice, have students complete Worktext p. 112.

Remind students that...

• word parts are base words, word endings, small words within compound words, prefixes, and suffixes.

• words can have more than one word part.

• they can use word parts to determine the meaning of a word.

Word List

clockwork	selective
confession	slingshot
gracefully	slumbering
misinformed	sorrowful
reweave	unprepared

Guide Practice

Use the Word List to guide practice with word structure. Write *clockwork, slumbering, unprepared,* and *gracefully.* Guide students as they break apart each word into its parts. Ask prompting questions, such as: Which word

has both a prefix and a word ending? (unprepared) Which word is a compound word? (clockwork) Which word has two suffixes? (gracefully) As students break apart each word, invite them to rewrite the word parts or to draw lines between the parts of the words. After discussing the meanings of the words and the word parts, ask students to use the words in sentences.

Follow the same procedure with the remaining words from the Word List.

If... students have difficulty identifying the word parts within a word,

then... remind them that a prefix comes before a word and changes the word's meaning, a suffix comes after a word and changes the word's meaning, and word endings come at the end of words.

On Their Own For additional practice with word structure, have students complete Worktext p. 113.

Vocabulary
Student Worktext

Name _____

1. Where are you?

2. Will you come to my party?

3. What is that?

4. Help me please.

5. Jake has a little brother.

6. I like your dress.

7. We saw many trees in the park.

8. Mark said to go that way.

 Directions Read one of the sentences aloud. Have your child find the sentence you read. Then have your child read a sentence aloud for you to find.

Vocabulary Lesson 1

where	**come**
what	**help**
little	**your**
many	**said**

1. Where could the bus be?

2. Take out your paper.

3. Many people eat here.

4. Where do you live?

5. There is a bird in the nest.

6. I need to work on my book report.

7. We could work together.

8. Apples are the best food.

 Directions Help your child cut some of the sentences into individual words. Have your child read each word to you in random order.

could

paper

people

live

there

work

together

food

1. Jake's little brother will grow.

2. I want to become a movie star.

3. Sam and I go around the park.

4. We always go this way.

5. Where is the water?

6. There are three people in his family.

7. Jen's family has a big house.

8. We were at the pool.

 Directions Randomly point to a word in one of the sentences. Have your child read the word to you. Repeat with other words.

grow	become
around	always
water	family
house	were

1. Sam has nothing to do.

2. It is time for school.

3. We go to school every day.

4. Do you have enough paper?

5. Laura has her own room.

6. Lisa and Tom read their books.

7. She wants everything in the store.

8. There is a tree outside our school.

 Directions Choose a word in one of the sentences. Have your child find that word written someplace else, such as in a newspaper, in a magazine, or on a food container.

nothing	**school**
every	**enough**
own	**their**
everything	**our**

Vocabulary Lesson 1

High-Frequency Words **9**

1. My friends are in the house.

2. The kitten is afraid of the water.

3. Dad likes to read the paper.

4. Let's watch the movie again.

5. I know what I want to do after school.

6. The food is done.

7. Where does your family live?

8. Jane said goodbye to her friends.

Copyright © Pearson Education, Inc., or its affiliates. All Rights Reserved.

Directions Ask your child to cut up the words in one of the sentences. Have your child put the words back together to make the sentence. Then have your child read the sentence to you. Repeat with other sentences.

Vocabulary Lesson 1

Name _____

friends	**afraid**
read	**again**
know	**done**
does	**goodbye**

1. They eat before school.

2. The rabbit won't go near the house.

3. Turn right when you see the school.

4. The dog won't come outside.

5. Would you come to my house?

6. Do not worry.

7. The book is about a family.

8. What does that sign say?

 Directions Secretly choose a word in one of the sentences. Spell the word aloud slowly. Have your child find the word and read the sentence to you.

Vocabulary Lesson 1

before	won't
right	surprise
would	worry
about	sign

1. Do you see the blue water?

2. My brother and I quickly ran home.

3. Tasha and I sat on the green grass.

4. Chris might go on a bike ride today.

5. The green truck is pulling the car.

6. Liz and Mark stood in the hall.

7. Ana has three older sisters.

8. Who is that woman?

Directions Read one of the sentences aloud. Ask your child to listen for one of the words on the word cards. After your child has selected the word he or she heard, ask him or her to read the sentence back to you.

blue	**quickly**
green	**might**
pulling	**stood**
three	**woman**

1. All my friends like to draw.

2. Please do not touch the art.

3. Of all the colors, Jim likes blue the most.

4. The airplane flew above the city.

5. I have a great surprise for you.

6. Mom took a picture of the family.

7. We eat together once a day.

8. I found my book.

School + Home **Directions** Ask your child to cut the sentences into individual words. Lay the words face down. Have your child pick words one at a time and read them to you.

draw

touch

colors

above

great

picture

once

found

1. Kevin sat alone in his room.

2. Mom works for a good company.

3. I play soccer five days a week.

4. Jon's family has four dogs.

5. Lee likes to sit in his large blue chair.

6. Ducks swim on the surface of the water.

7. They go under the water to get food.

8. We can eat whatever you like.

School + Home **Directions** Choose a word from one of the sentences. Give your child clues to guess the word. For example, *This word has four letters. It begins with the letter ___. It rhymes with ___.*

18 High-Frequency Words   **Vocabulary Lesson 1**

alone	**company**
five	**four**
large	**surface**
under	**whatever**

1. Jill and I took the bus into town.

2. I laugh with my friends.

3. We thought it would rain.

4. Do you remember me?

5. Jason has only a blue pen.

6. My school is across from my house.

7. Sam ran quickly because of the rain.

8. I opened the door.

Directions Say a word from one of the sentences and have your child spell it for you. Then have your child read the sentence that includes the word.

Vocabulary Lesson 1

took

laugh

thought

remember

only

across

because

opened

1. My mom put on her shoes.

2. Her friends were behind the house.

3. They came toward the house.

4. We opened the door.

5. Pam has brown eyes.

6. She loved the surprise.

7. We sat among our friends.

8. I want this cookie instead of that one.

 Directions Have your child copy the sentences on a separate piece of paper. Then have him or her read the sentences to you.

Vocabulary Lesson 1

shoes	behind
toward	door
eyes	loved
among	instead

1. Jess goes to another school.

2. None of them said goodbye.

3. He goes to the park every day.

4. It is too early to go to school.

5. He leans against the door.

6. That bag is heavy.

7. I have a surprise for you today.

8. What should I do now?

 Directions Say a word from one of the sentences. Ask your child to spell the word.

Name _____

another

goes

early

against

heavy

today

should

1. He lives in a different country.

2. The people built a new house.

3. I like to learn new things.

4. My sister wants to learn about science.

5. The children ran through the house.

6. No one answered the door.

7. The flowers are beautiful.

8. This flower is different from that one.

 Directions Read one of the sentences aloud. Have your child find the sentence you read. Then have him or her read a sentence for you to find.

　　　　　　　　　　　　　Vocabulary Lesson 1

country	**built**
learn	**science**
through	**answered**
beautiful	**different**

1. Will someone please answer the door?

2. My shoes are somewhere in the house.

3. I have looked everywhere.

4. There is a sign above the machines.

5. Could you please move this heavy sign?

6. Would you like to travel around the world?

7. Sam and Van could build a house.

8. They couldn't be late for school.

 Directions Have your child cut up a few of the sentences into individual words. Have your child read each word to you in random order.

someone	somewhere
everywhere	machines
move	world
build	couldn't

1. My friends are gone.

2. Kate wants to learn more about animals.

3. We often come here.

4. I cut my food into little pieces.

5. Dad likes the house even though it is small.

6. Do not break the machines.

7. I heard someone at the door.

8. Listen as I play the drum.

 Directions Randomly point to a word in one of the sentences. Have your child read the word to you. Repeat with other words.

Name _____

gone

animals

often

pieces

though

break

heard

listen

Vocabulary Lesson 1

1. Either one is good to eat.

2. The storm was the worst we have had.

3. You're very good at science.

4. Our whole family lives here.

5. My friend bought food for the animals.

6. My mother brought me to school.

7. Everybody brought a few friends.

8. Please wait here for one minute.

 Directions Choose a word in one of the sentences. Have your child find that word written someplace else, such as in a newspaper, in a magazine, or on a food container.

Vocabulary Lesson 1

either	**worst**
you're	**whole**
bought	**brought**
everybody	**minute**

Name _____

1. We finally found my dog!

2. Where have you been?

3. Guess what I learned today.

4. I believe you are right.

5. My friend caught a cold.

6. Will you go to school tomorrow?

7. I ate half of the sandwich.

8. Our neighbor moved to a different house.

 Directions Write a word from one of the sentences in large letters on paper. Have your child outline the letters of the word several times. Ask your child to name each letter as it is outlined and then read the word. Repeat with other words.

Vocabulary Lesson 1

finally	been
caught	tomorrow
guess	believe
half	neighbor

1. Her parents want to buy a new house.

2. There are four daughters in the family.

3. I am the youngest in my family.

4. My mother bought my new clothes.

5. I am in school for many hours every day.

6. She has money for a new book.

7. May I ask you a question?

8. My sister taught me the rules of the game.

Directions Say a word from one of the sentences and have your child spell it for you.

buy	**daughters**
youngest	**clothes**
hours	**money**
question	**taught**

1. I sit between my friends at the lunch table.

2. Sara covered her locker with pictures.

3. Tim's dog likes following him around the park.

4. Paul wants to measure how fast he runs.

5. We used to live near the mountains.

6. I promised to take my little brother to the game.

7. Victor got second place in the race.

8. Sometimes my family eats outside.

 Directions Choose a word in one of the sentences. Have your child find that word written someplace else, such as in a newspaper, in a magazine, or on a food container.

between

covered

following

measure

mountains

promised

second

sometimes

1. In the beginning of the story, Jack finds a map.

2. I decided to play soccer instead of baseball.

3. Rafi has an important test today.

4. People lived here thousands of years ago.

5. It seemed like night because the sky was so dark.

6. Please write a sentence to answer the question.

7. Rose drew a straight line on her paper.

8. I usually read a book before bed.

 Directions Randomly point to a word in one of the sentences. Have your child read the word to you. Repeat with other words.

beginning	**decided**
important	**thousands**
seemed	**sentence**
straight	**usually**

Name _____

Read each word.
Draw a line between the two small words.
Write one of the words on the line.

1. **backpack:** _____ for your back

2. **teapot:** pot for _____

3. **rowboat:** boat you _____

4. **goldfish:** fish that is _____

5. **bedtime:** _____ for bed

6. **raincoat:** coat for the _____

7. **playpen:** _____ for play

8. **airplane:** plane that flies in the _____

9. **sandbox:** box of _____

10. **popcorn:** _____ that you pop

11. **bedroom:** room with a _____

 Directions Have your child read the words and the meanings for them. Then take turns using the words in sentences.

　　　　　　　　　　　　　Vocabulary Lesson 2

Name _____

Read the words.
Match a word in List 1 with a word in List 2 to make a compound word.
Write the compound words on the lines.

List 1	List 2	
1. basket	way	_____
2. high	drum	_____
3. home	card	_____
4. chalk	work	_____
5. ear	ball	_____
6. post	board	_____
7. down	bug	_____
8. lady	fly	_____
9. fire	cake	_____
10. cup	town	_____

Directions Have your child read each compound word he or she wrote and then tell you the two words that make up the compound word. Take turns using the words in sentences.

Name _____

Read the sentences.
Write a word from the Word Bank to complete the compound word.

ground	watch	ball	quake	eye
shot	pour	spread	run	wheel

1. I always use a _____ point pen to do my homework.

2. Sarah's favorite gift is the bed_____ that her aunt made.

3. The airplane landed on the _____way.

4. The earth_____ made the house shake for thirty seconds.

5. The lake was a beautiful back_____ for the family photo.

6. In her new _____chair, Grandma can go more places.

7. Jake used a stop_____ to time his lap around the track.

8. Sara got stuck in a down_____ and came home soaking wet.

9. If you find an _____lash, blow it off your finger and make a wish.

10. Kate hung a snap_____ of her dog in her locker.

Directions Have your child read each sentence to you. Then talk with him or her about the meaning of each compound word.

Name _____

Read the sentences.
Circle the word of the color that correctly completes each sentence.
Write the words.
Describe the picture.

1. The sky is _____.   (brown)   (blue)

2. The apple is _____.   (red)   (blue)

3. The grass is _____.   (green)   (white)

4. The clouds are _____.   (brown)   (white)

5. The leaves are _____.   (white)   (green)

6. The squirrels are _____.   (green)   (brown)

Directions In school, your child learned to give descriptions using words for colors. Ask your child to read the sentences to you. Then, with your child, describe a recent trip to a park. Encourage him or her to give many details, using descriptive words.

Name _____

Pick three of the words below.
Give a description of a person, place, or thing using the words you chose.

above	**beneath**	**beside**
eager	**grumpy**	**loud**
quiet	**relaxed**	**shy**
sudden	**full**	**empty**

Directions In school, your child gave descriptions using these words. With your child, pick three random cards. Ask your child to describe a real or imaginary event using the words on the cards you chose. Encourage your child to provide details in his or her description.

46 Descriptive Words

Name _____

Read the sentences.
Use words from the Word Bank to complete the sentences.
Write sentences to continue the description.

cautious	fierce	enormous	dangerous
shimmering	murky	charming	
lively	amazing	peculiar	

1. Yesterday, something _____ happened.

2. My friend Jack and I were sitting by the _____ lake.

3. Jack noticed a _____ coyote crouching near the water.

4. The coyote looked _____.

5. Then it stood up quickly, and Jack said, "Let's be _____."

I said, "_____

_____."

Jack and I _____

_____

Directions In school, your child learned to give detailed descriptions using descriptive words. Help your child use the words from the Word Bank to complete the paragraph. Then ask your child to describe what happens next. Take turns reading aloud the paragraph.

Read the words in the box at the bottom of the page.

Sort the words into two groups.

Write the name of each group at the top of the chart. **Then write** the words in the appropriate column of the chart.

_____	_____
_____	_____
_____	_____
_____	_____
_____	_____

breakfast	snow	summer	store	snack
spring	school	rain	dinner	wind
winter	lunch	heat	home	farm

Directions Ask your child to name the groups he or she made and to tell you why the words belong in each group. Then discuss with your child other groups that could be made from the set of words.

Vocabulary Lesson 4

Read each word. **Cut** out the word cards.
Sort the word cards into groups.

river	canyon	stream	volcano
mountain	waterfall	island	plain
forest	prairie	ocean	field
hill	desert	creek	valley

Directions In school, your child learned to sort words into groups. Pick a card at random. Ask your child to create a group that includes that word. Ask him or her which words fit in the group and why.

Read each word in the box below. **Then read** the group names in the chart.
Write each word in the correct column of the chart.
Use a dictionary to find the definitions for words you do not know.

alligator	salmon	elk	antelope	guppy
cougar	cobra	minnow	beagle	bass
llama	rattlesnake	walrus	hog	crocodile

Mammal	Reptile	Fish

Directions In school, your child discussed how to sort the list of words into groups. Ask your child to read the words for you, sort them, and explain the groups he or she made.

Vocabulary Lesson 4

Read the words.
Cut out the cards.
Match pairs of words that are opposites.

long	**tiny**	**left**
down	**short**	**hot**
right	**huge**	**bad**
good	**cold**	**up**

Directions In school, your child learned about antonyms, or words for opposites. Pick a card at random and ask your child to read it. Then ask him or her to find the word with an opposite meaning.

Name _____

Read the underlined words.
Circle the antonym of the underlined word in the sentence next to it.

1. <u>answer</u> Can I ask you a question?

_____

2. <u>leave</u> I arrive at school every morning at the same time.

_____

3. <u>float</u> The stone will sink in the water.

_____

4. <u>break</u> Jane needs to fix her bike.

_____

5. <u>begin</u> Please finish cleaning your room.

_____

6. <u>small</u> We sat around the big table.

_____

7. <u>sad</u> Ana was happy to see her brother.

_____

8. <u>short</u> The tall man turned on the fan.

_____

Directions In school, your child learned about antonyms, or words for opposites. Have your child read each sentence to you. Then help your child write a sentence for each underlined word.

Name _____

Read the sentences.
Write the bold word's antonym on the line below it.

future	loser	ancient	cautious
dawn	expensive	forget	

1. At **sundown**, Mark and Jake lit the campfire.

_____

2. Today Marie learned about **old** railroads in the United States.

_____

3. The **champion** of the team grinned and held the trophy in the air.

_____

4. Last week we went to the museum to look at **modern** art.

_____

5. As he was dusting, Drew was **careless** and knocked a vase off the shelf.

_____

6. The movie theater near my house sells **cheap** tickets.

_____

7. Please **remember** to turn off the lights before you go to bed.

_____

Directions In school, your child learned about antonyms, or words for opposites. Have your child read the sentences to you. Then take turns making up sentences that include the words from the Word Bank.

Name _____

Add the prefix to the base word.
Write the new word on the line.
Draw a line to the picture that matches the sentence.

1. uni + cycle

A _____ has one wheel.

2. bi + cycle

A _____ has two wheels.

3. tri + cycle

A _____ has three wheels.

4. tri + angle   _____

5. semi + circle   _____

6. hemi + sphere   _____

School + Home **Directions** In school, your child learned how Greek and Latin prefixes change the meanings of words. Ask your child to read the words, tell you what each prefix means, and then use the prefix to tell the meaning of the word.

Vocabulary Lesson 6

Add the prefix to the word.
Write the new word on the line.
Read the sentences.

1. sub + marine

A _____ goes below water.

2. sub + zero

_____ means "below zero."

3. co + pilots

_____ fly together.

4. co + workers

_____ work together.

5. super + man

A _____ is stronger than an average man.

6. super + star

A _____ is a big star.

7. inter + view

An _____ is a talk between people.

8. inter + state

An _____ goes between states.

 Directions Ask your child to read the words and tell what each prefix means. Then with your child, think of other sentences that include these words.

Name _____

Read the sentences.

Add -logy, -logist, or **-ist** to complete the words.

1. A **bio**_____ studies living things.

2. An **art**_____ makes art.

3. The study of animals is called **zoo**_____.

4. A **novel**_____ writes novels, or books.

5. A **zoo**_____ studies animals.

6. The study of living things is called **bio**_____.

7. A **dent**_____ does dental work, or works with teeth.

8. An **eco**_____ studies nature.

9. A **journal**_____ writes for newspapers or journals.

10. The study of nature is called **eco**_____.

11. A **violin**_____ plays the violin.

Directions In school, your child learned about Latin and Greek affixes, or word parts. Ask your child to read each sentence and explain the meanings of the suffixes *-logist*, *-ist*, and *-logy*.

56 Greek/Latin Affixes

Vocabulary Lesson 6

Add the root to the word. **Write** the word they form.
Draw a line to the picture that shows the new word.

tele = far	*tract* = pull	*astr* = star

1. tele + phone _____

2. tele + vision _____

3. tele + scope _____

4. astro + naut _____

5. at + **tract** _____

School + Home **Directions** In school, your child learned about Greek and Latin roots. Read the words with your child. Talk with him or her about how each root affects the word's meaning.

Name _____

Read each sentence.
Choose the root that completes the word in each sentence.
Write the root.

scrib = write	*script* = written	*port* = carry

1. When you write a story, remember to de_____e the setting.

2. Liz asked the hotel _____er to carry her bag.

3. Jen's little sister _____bled on the wall with a pink marker.

4. If the tree house in my backyard was _____able, I would carry it to my new house.

5. Bob has written a _____ for the school talent show.

6. Most bananas in the United States are im_____ed from other countries.

7. All my grades from school are written in my tran_____.

8. This train will trans_____ coal across the country.

School + Home **Directions** In school, your child learned about Greek and Latin roots. Read the sentences with your child. Then take turns thinking of other words with the roots *scrib, script,* and *port*.

Find the word with the Latin root *dict, spect,* or *rupt* in each sentence.
Circle the root.
Write the word next to its meaning.

dict = speak	*spect* = see	*rupt* = break

1. Be sure to use good diction when you give your speech.

_____: *way of speaking or word choice*

2. The fireworks were an amazing spectacle.

_____: *an eye-catching sight*

3. The volcano might erupt any day.

_____: *break out or release suddenly*

4. Tanisha will dictate her ideas, and Sam will write them down.

_____: *to speak out loud to be recorded*

Directions In school, your child learned about the Latin roots *dict, spect,* and *rupt.* Ask him or her to explain to you which words have Latin roots and tell you what the words mean.

Name _____

Label each picture by writing its homonym from the chart below.
Draw a line between homonyms.

calf	pen	ring	fly

_____

_____

_____

_____

_____

_____

_____

_____

School + Home **Directions** In school, your child learned about homonyms, or words that sound the same but have different meanings. Take turns with your child thinking of sentences that include each homonym above.

60 Homonyms

Vocabulary Lesson 8

Read the sentences.
Underline the homonyms.
Circle the sentence that goes with the picture.

1. This key opens the back door.
   Every piano key is out of tune.

2. At the zoo we saw a bird with a purple bill.
   Helen found a five-dollar bill in her pocket.

3. The pupil is the dark center of the eye.
   One pupil left class.

4. The tennis match will be over soon.
   Use this match to light the grill.

5. Rob filled the pitcher with orange juice.
   The pitcher threw a fastball.

 Directions Ask your child to read the sentences and point out the homonyms. With your child, think of even more meanings of these words. For example, a *bill* is also a document that shows how much money you owe.

Name _____

Read the sentences.
Choose the correct meaning of the bold word from the chart at the bottom and write it below the sentence.

1. At the farm, we fed corn to the chickens and saw pigs eat from their bins. We watched the cows **graze** in the fields.

_____

2. When Mark lifted the flowerpot, he was startled to see hundreds of **bugs**.

_____

3. After hitting the target three times in a row, Diana took her **quiver** off her back and smiled.

_____

4. Jim asked the **groom** for help putting on the saddle.

_____

5. The movie's **plot** is about two friends who love to sing.

_____

1.	touch something while moving	eat grass or plants
2.	insects without wings	mistakes in a computer program
3.	a case for holding arrows	shake with cold or fear
4.	person who cares for horses	a man who is getting married
5.	piece of land	events in a story

 Directions Ask your child to read each sentence and talk about the bold word. With your child, think of sentences that use the alternate meaning of each homonym.

Name _____

Read the pairs of words.
Circle the words that go with each picture.

1. money bank   river bank

2. bed for sleep   bed for flowers

3. baseball bat   flying bat

4. coat of paint   winter coat

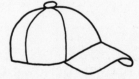

5. baseball cap   toothpaste cap

6. tree bark   dog bark

Directions In school, your child learned about words that mean more than one thing. Read each phrase with your child. Ask him or her to tell you which phrase matches the picture. Then take turns thinking of sentences that include each multiple-meaning word.

Name _____

Read each sentence.
Circle the bold word's meaning.

1. Let's take a **break** and sit down.

   rest

   crack or split

2. The flashlight had a bright **beam**.

   large bar of wood

   ray of light

3. The sky was **clear**.

   not cloudy

   easy to understand

4. Jake had a **float** for desert.

   moving car at a parade

   soda with ice cream

5. Ben fixed his jeans with a **patch**.

   fabric to cover a hole

   area to grow food

6. Aunt Liz owns her own **company**.

   visitors

   business

Directions In school, your child learned about words that have more than one meaning. Ask your child to read each sentence and to tell you the meaning of the bold word as it is used in the sentence. Then take turns creating sentences that use a different meaning of the word.

Vocabulary Lesson 9

Name _____

Read the sentences and the meanings. **Write** the bold word's meaning under each sentence.

1. Use the **blade** to open the box.

_____

2. Sally likes to **trace** her name in the sand.

_____

3. The team practiced a running **drill**.

_____

4. There will be snow, sleet, and **negative** temperatures today.

_____

5. On the day of the test, Ann wore a **charm** around her neck.

_____

1.	sharp edge	piece of grass
2.	draw	small amount
3.	repeated action	tool to make holes
4.	below zero	bad
5.	object for luck	likeable quality

Directions In school, your child learned about words with multiple meanings. Ask your child to read each sentence and tell you which definition is correct. Then make up sentences with your child using the other definitions for the bold words.

Name _____

Add the prefix to the base word.
Write the new word.
Talk about the word.

1. dis + like   _____

2. un + lock   _____

3. mis + use   _____

4. un + pin   _____

5. mis + place   _____

6. un + do   _____

7. dis + trust   _____

8. un + zip   _____

Directions In school, your child added prefixes to base words to make new words. Read each word with your child. Ask him or her to tell you what the prefix and the new word mean.

66 Prefixes *un-, dis-, mis-*   **Vocabulary Lesson 10**

Name _____

Add the prefix to the base word.
Write the new word on the first line.
Write the base word on the second line.
Write a sentence using the new word.

1. dis + agree

_____ means "to not _____."

_____

2. dis + believe

_____ means "to not _____."

_____

3. un + cover

_____ means "the opposite of _____."

_____

4. mis + place

_____ means "to put in the wrong _____."

_____

5. mis + copy

_____ means "to not _____ correctly."

_____

Directions In school, your child added prefixes to base words. Ask your child to read each word and then read the sentence they wrote for each new word they built.

Name _____

Add the prefix to the base word. **Write** the new word below.
Write the word's meaning in the box next to it. **Choose** from the definitions
at the bottom.

1. mis + pronounce

_____

2. dis + respect

_____

3. dis + advantage

_____

4. dis + prove

_____

5. un + aware

_____

difficulty or weakness
to say incorrectly
lack of respect
not knowing about something
to show that something is not true

Directions Ask your child to read each word and talk about the word's meaning. Ask him or
her how the word's prefix changes each word. Then take turns using the word in a sentence.

Copyright © Pearson Education, Inc., or its affiliates. All Rights Reserved.

Vocabulary Lesson 10

Read the sentences.
Fill in the missing prefix or the missing part of the meaning.

pre-	before
re-	again

1. **Preheat** means "heat _____."

2. **Rename** means "name _____."

3. _____**tell** means "tell _____again_____."

4. _____**set** means "set _____before_____."

5. _____**use** means "use _____again_____."

6. **Repack** means "pack _____."

7. **Prepay** means "pay _____."

8. **Redraw** means "draw _____."

School + Home **Directions** In school, your child learned about the prefixes *pre-* and *re-*. Ask your child to read each word and meaning. Then take turns creating sentences that include each word.

Name _____

Add **pre** to sentences 1–4. **Add re** to sentences 5–9.
Read the sentences.
Write the new word.
Tell what the new word means.

1. This city _____dates the Civil War.   _____

2. As a _____caution, always wear a bike helmet.   _____

3. Alex tried not to _____judge the man next door.   _____

4. I like watching the _____views before a movie.   _____

5. Now the rabbit will _____appear in the hat!   _____

6. Joe broke Bill's video game and has to
_____place it.   _____

7. Jess tried to _____discover the cave using an   _____
old map.

8. After the soccer game, the coaches set a   _____
_____match for next week.

9. The school has to _____order more paper for   _____
the printers.

Directions In school, your child learned how to add prefixes to words. Ask your child to tell you the meanings of the words he or she wrote above.

70 Prefixes *pre-, re-*   **Vocabulary Lesson 11**

Name _____

Read the sentences.
Find a word from the Word Bank that completes each sentence.
Write the new word.

mature	attach	program	phrase	capture
create	write	season	historic	

1. Too much sun can cause pre_____ skin damage.

_____

2. For the set of the play, we have to re_____ the Wild West.

_____

3. Mom asked Dad to pre_____ the TV to record the news.

_____

4. Liza used a roll of tape to re_____ her posters to the wall.

_____

5. Can you please re_____ the question?

_____

6. Today Sue learned about pre_____ animals, like dinosaurs.

_____

 Directions Ask your child to read each sentence to you. Ask him or her to explain how the prefixes *pre-* and *re-* affect the meanings of the words.

Name _____

Read the words.
Find the root word.
Write the root word on the line.

1. replay   _____

2. ending   _____

3. working   _____

4. painting   _____

5. unending   _____

6. repaint   _____

7. redo   _____

8. playing   _____

9. relearn   _____

10. reread   _____

Directions In school, your child found root words, or base words. Ask your child to read the words to you. Then take turns thinking of more words that share these root words.

Vocabulary Lesson 12

Read the words.
Circle the root words.
Use the root words to finish the puzzle.

Across

1. uncorrected

2. breakable

3. unchanged

Down

1. relock

2. centered

Name _____

Read the sentences.
Circle the root word.
Write the definition of the bold word.

1. Kelly is raising money to start a school for <u>uneducated</u> children.

    uneducated: _____

2. There is a lot of traffic because of the <u>construction</u> near the highway.

    construction: _____

3. When the storm started, Mom began <u>disconnecting</u> the TV, microwave, and radio.

    disconnecting: _____

the act of building	without education or teaching
to teach or give information	breaking the connection between
to move suddenly out of fear	to build

School + Home **Directions** Ask your child to read each sentence to you. Have your child identify the root word of each underlined word. Then take turns thinking of more words that have the root words *educate*, *construct*, and *connect*.

Vocabulary Lesson 12

Name _____

Read the sentence.
Decide whether **–ful** or **–less** makes sense in the blank.
Write **–ful** or **–less** on the line.

1. The use_____ broken toy sat on the shelf.

2. Be care_____ with that box of glasses!

3. Sam was care_____ and broke the cup.

4. Thanks for being so help_____ today.

5. Jon felt hope_____ and sad.

6. Baby birds are help_____.

7. David felt thank_____ for the wonderful gift.

8. The dog was hope_____ it would get a treat after doing tricks.

9. Even though Ms. Jo did thank_____ work, she always did her work with a smile.

10. This new hammer works great and is very use_____!

Directions In school, your child learned about the suffixes *-ful* and *-less*. Ask your child to read the sentences to you. Then take turns thinking of more words that share these suffixes.

Vocabulary Lesson 13   Suffixes *-ful*, *-less* **75**

Name _____

Read the sentences.
Circle the correct suffix.
Write the new word.

1. The snake looked scary was but was really harm_____ .

| ful | less |

_____

2. Jim likes doing mind_____ things like watch the clouds.

| ful | less |

_____

3. The power_____ king told everyone what to do.

| ful | less |

_____

4. Please be mind_____ of the signs so we do not get lost.

| ful | less |

_____

5. Amy felt rest_____ and uneasy.

| ful | less |

_____

6. Too much sun is harm_____ to some plants.

| ful | less |

_____

7. Ron wanted to help but felt power_____ .

| ful | less |

_____

Name _____

Read the sentences.
Add –ful or **–less** to one of the words in the box below to finish each sentence.

doubt	meaning	grace	flavor	thought

1. Juan loved every bite of the _____ meal.

2. After losing the contest, Brian felt his hard work had been
_____.

3. The dancer looked _____ as she moved smoothly across the stage.

4. Rita was _____ that forgetful Rachel would give back her book.

5. Jack was _____ and called Jon on his birthday.

6. Lana thought the dancers looked clumsy and _____.

7. Chris had a long and _____ talk with his Grandpa.

8. That cake was the most _____ cake I have ever eaten!

9. Sue was _____ and talked loudly about her party in front of people who were not invited.

10. When I am sick, anything I eat tastes _____.

 Directions Ask your child to read each sentence to you. Have him or her tell you what each of the words mean.

Name _____

Write the suffix.
Write the new words.

–ly

1. neat_____   _____

2. sad_____   _____

3. loud_____   _____

4. nice_____   _____

5. help_____   _____

–al

6. coast_____   _____

7. accident_____   _____

8. education_____   _____

9. music_____   _____

10. person_____   _____

School + Home **Directions** Have your child add the suffixes -*ly* and -*al* to these base words and roots. Ask your child to read the words to you. Then take turns thinking of sentences with these words.

Vocabulary Lesson 14

Add –ly to sentences 1–5. **Add –al** to sentences 6–10.
Write the new word to finish each sentence.

HINT: The base words *globe* and *nature* lose their *e* when you add **–al.**

1. accident + **al**

The discovery of gold in this town was _____.

2. person + **al**

David does not like people touching his _____ things.

3. natur(e) + **al**

In science class Jeff learns about the _____ world.

4. nation + **al**

Our _____ flag is red, white, and blue.

5. bright + **ly**

Andrea and I went into the _____ lit room.

7. slow + **ly**

The turtle _____ came out of its shell.

8. proud + **ly**

Anita's mom _____ watched her give the speech.

9. glob(e) + **al**

Today Ms. Parker talked about _____ warming.

 Directions Ask your child to read each sentence. Ask him or her to tell you the meanings of the words he or she wrote.

Name _____

Read the sentences.
Add –ly or **–al** to one of the words to finish each sentence.
Write the new word.

1. Pete put on his warm hat and walked brisk_____ to school.

_____

2. Alice's favorite cultur(e)_____ place is the modern art museum.

_____

3. Jacob rough_____ pushed past Sam.

_____

4. When I grow up, I want to be a profession_____ writer.

_____

5. Ron's dad said he would pick him up at precise_____ eight o'clock.

_____

6. The weather report said there will be occasion_____ showers.

_____

7. This candy is artificial_____ flavored.

_____

8. The experiment_____ data shows that the scientists have to run more tests.

_____

School + Home **Directions** Read each sentence with your child. Ask him or her to tell you what each word means.

80 Suffixes -*ly, -al*   **Vocabulary Lesson 14**

Name _____

Add –ness to each word.
Draw a line to the word's meaning.

1. dark_____   state of being dry

2. kind_____   state of being dark

3. dry_____   state of being loud

4. loud_____   state of being kind

5. cold_____   state of being glad

6. shy_____   state of being cold

7. glad_____   state of being shy

8. sick_____   state of being sick

9. good_____   state of being fair

10. soft_____   state of being good

11. fair_____   state of being soft

School + Home **Directions** Ask your child to tell you the meaning of each word. Then take turns using the words in sentences.

Name _____

Add **–ness** to 1–4. **Add –ion** to 5–8.
Write the new word to finish each sentence.

1. gentle_____

The _____ of the lion playing with its cub surprised us.

2. aware_____

Jeff wants to raise school _____ about recycling.

3. bold_____

Maria liked the _____ of the painting's colors.

4. bright_____

The _____ of the lamp hurt Sean's eyes.

5. direct_____

Are we going in the right _____?

6. collect_____

Patrick has a large _____ of books.

7. erupt_____

There was an _____ of applause from the audience after Anita gave the speech.

8. correct_____

Today the school paper printed a _____.

 Directions Ask your child to read each sentence. Ask him or her to tell you the meanings of the words he or she wrote.

82 Suffixes *-ness, -ion*

Vocabulary Lesson 15

Name _____

Add –ness to the first group of words. **Add –ion** to the second group of words. **Write** the words in the sentences.

shallow_____   **awkward**_____   **blind**_____

1. The _____ of the water let us see the small fish at the bottom of the river.

2. There was some _____ between the step-brothers when they first met.

3. The poet John Milton could not see. He wrote a poem about his

_____.

translat(e)_____   **creat(e)**_____   **instruct**_____

HINT: Drop the final *e* of two words before adding **ion**.

1. The class read a _____ of a French story.

2. When Ms. Joan gives an _____, everyone listens.

3. The _____ of a school swimming club would help all students have fun and be healthy.

Directions Read each sentence with your child. Ask him or her to tell you what each word means.

Name _____

Add –able to each word.
Write the new word to complete the phrase.
Read the phrases.

1. wash_____   _____ shirt

2. sink_____   _____ boat

3. trac(e)_____   _____ footprint

4. lik(e)_____   _____ person

5. comfort_____   _____ bed

6. enjoy_____   _____ party

7. read_____   _____ sign

8. accept_____   _____ decision

9. learn_____   _____ skill

10. break_____   _____ vase

Directions Ask your child to read each word and tell you its meaning. Then take turns reading the phrases.

Name _____

Add –able to the first list. **Add –ive** to the second list.
Write the new word to finish each sentence.

able   **ive**

adapt_____   act_____

return_____   attract_____

question_____   secret_____

understand_____   creat(e)_____

reason_____   support_____

1. Paul plays many sports and is an _____ person. (act)

2. Ann thinks about things carefully. She is _____. (reason)

3. Chris was _____ when planning the surprise party. (secret)

4. Sara is a very _____ worker. (depend)

5. My new jacket has a hole. I am glad it is _____. (return)

6. Becca is a _____ artist who sings and paints. (create)

 Directions Ask your child to read each word and tell you its meaning. Take turns reading the sentences. Then help your child think of sentences using the remaining words from the lists.

Name _____

Read the sentences. **Add** –able or –ive to the words.
Write the new word.

-able = *can be*	*-ive* = *likely to*

1. A **respect**_____ person can be respected.

_____

2. An **invent**_____ person is likely to invent.

_____

3. Reflect_____ glass is likely to reflect.

_____

4. Recycl(e)_____ bottles can be recycled.

_____

5. Adjust_____ straps can be adjusted.

_____

Directions Read each sentence with your child. Ask him or her to tell you what the bold words mean. With your child, think of other words that end with *–able* or *–ive*.

Add –ish to each word.
Write the new word on the line.
Read the phrase.

1. round_____   _____ shape

2. tall_____   _____ man

3. new_____   _____ bike

4. green_____   _____ light

5. long_____   _____ line

6. child_____   _____ joke

7. boy_____   _____ laugh

8. sick_____   _____ feeling

9. fool_____   _____ act

10. small_____   _____ room

Directions Ask your child to read each word and tell you its meaning. Then take turns making up more phrases or sentences for each of the words.

Name _____

Read each word with the suffix added.
Write the new word to finish each sentence.

HINT: Some base words drop the final *e* when you add a suffix.

1. fever + **ish**

I feel sick and _____.

2. fam(e) + **ous**

Lee wants to be rich and _____ when he is older.

3. young + **ish**

Tamara's new teacher is _____ and has curly hair.

4. kitten + **ish**

My old cat looks _____ when she plays with string.

5. yellow + **ish**

The walls used to be white, but now they are _____.

6. mountain + **ous**

Jack likes to go hiking in _____ areas.

 Directions Have your child add the suffixes *-ous* or *-ish* to the words and write the words in the sentences. Ask your child to read the words and sentences. Then ask your child to tell you what each word means.

Name _____

Add –ish to 1–3. **Add –ous** to 4–6.

Write the new word to complete the sentence.

HINT: Some base words drop the final *e* when you add a suffix.

1. styl(e)_____

Tommy thinks he is _____, but his clothes are terrible.

2. nightmar(e)_____

The _____ movie was so scary that I closed my eyes.

3. sheep_____

In the story, the _____ boy learned to be strong.

4. humor_____

The school play was _____ and made everybody laugh.

5. virtu(e)_____

My _____ Aunt Liz gives most of her money to charity.

Vocabulary Lesson 17   Suffixes *-ous, -ish* **89**

Name _____

Cut out the cards.
Read the words.
Group the synonyms together.

big	fast	small	huge
neat	little	quick	tug
drag	clean	large	speak
speedy	say	tidy	talk

School + Home **Directions** In school, your child learned about synonyms, or words that have similar meanings. Ask your child to read the words. Then have him or her explain which words have similar meanings.

Read the sentences.
Circle the synonym of the underlined word that is also in the sentence.
Write the two words on the lines.

1. Archita is <u>smart</u>, and her cousin is clever too.

_____   _____

2. Al took a <u>journey</u> just like the voyage his father took many years before.

_____   _____

3. I like to look for clues to solve a <u>puzzle</u>. Rob also likes solving a mystery.

_____   _____

4. Everyone at the game tried to <u>yell</u> or shout the loudest.

_____   _____

5. Whatever ice cream flavor I <u>choose</u>, Jane will also select that flavor.

_____   _____

6. When you sleep over, we have a <u>spare</u> bed and extra pillows you can use.

_____   _____

Directions In school, your child learned about synonyms, or words that have the same or almost the same meaning. Read each sentence with your child. Ask him or her which words are synonyms. Then take turns thinking of more synonyms for the words.

Name _____

Read the sentences. **Circle** the synonym of the underlined word in the sentence.
Choose another synonym from the Word Bank. **Write** the word.

section	present	timid	observes	blunders	rowdy

1. Abbey <u>sees</u> a cat in the window, and Lisa notices the cat too.

_____

2. The museum will <u>exhibit</u> old paintings. It will also display newer art.

_____

3. Rachel is very quiet and <u>shy</u>, but her best friend is not bashful at all.

_____

4. I made no <u>mistakes</u> on the last test, so I want no errors on this test too.

_____

5. The plate broke. Mike picked up a <u>piece</u>, and Van picked up a fragment too.

_____

6. The children began running everywhere and acting <u>wild</u>. Mrs. Parson was
shocked by their unruly behavior.

_____

 Directions Read each sentence with your child. Ask him or her to tell you which words are
synonyms, or words that have nearly the same meanings. Then talk about the meanings of the
words in the Word Bank.

Name _____

Read the sentences.
Circle the clue word or words for the meaning of the word in bold.

1. Todd lives in a **cottage**, or little house.

2. Tara saw a **skiff**, or small boat, on the water.

3. We drove on the **freeway**, which means big road.

4. A **puma**–that is a big wild cat–lives in the woods.

5. The pig used its **snout**, or nose, to find food.

6. There is a big **mound**, or hill, near the school.

7. We ate **rye**, which is a kind of bread, for lunch.

8. My sister drew a **pansy**, which is a small flower.

9. Bryan put on his **parka**, or big coat.

10. A **mallard**, which is a kind of duck, lives in the pond.

Directions In school, your child learned how to figure out meanings of words by looking for clue words that signal that there are definitions in a sentence. Read the sentences with your child. Then take turns making up other definitions for the bold words.

Name _____

Read the sentences.
Read the meanings.
Write the meanings under the matching bold words.

a kind of sickness	fresh fruits and vegetables	a long, light sled
a large and special dinner	to cook in an oven or over fire	to cry because of sadness

1. Josh ate enough food for a week during the two-hour **banquet.**

_____

2. I asked Mary not to **weep**, but the tears ran down her face.

_____

3. People who get **mumps** have a fever and a sore throat.

_____

4. Tyrone loves winter because he gets to ride his **toboggan** down the hills near his house.

_____

5. We bought peas, lettuce, grapes, and other **produce** at the market.

_____

6. Drew wants to **roast** chicken and bake potatoes for dinner.

_____

Directions In school, your child learned how to use the words around an unfamiliar word to figure out the meaning of the unfamiliar word. Ask your child to read the sentences. Then ask how he or she figured out the meaning of each bold word.

Vocabulary Lesson 19

Read the sentences.
Circle the words in the box that tell what the underlined word means.

1. Frank is a <u>competent</u> worker. He always shows up to work on time. While he works, he never lets his mind wander. Frank keeps his desk neat and organized.

able to do a job well	extremely smart	without energy

2. Almost every person in the <u>procession</u> held a sign. We watched the long line of people walk slowly down the street. The people in the line went on for a mile.

a long road where people travel	an organized group of moving people or cars

3. Mrs. Lee is a <u>consistent</u> supporter of our school who we can always count on.

rich or wealthy	always acting in the same way	fun to be around

4. The <u>clamor</u> in the town hall meeting came as a surprise to the mayor. He did not realize how upset the community was about two parks being torn down. He had a hard time talking above all the yelling.

emptiness	peaceful silence	shouting that is very loud

Directions Your child learned to figure out the meaning of an unfamiliar word by reading the words and sentences around it. Take turns finding the clues that show the meanings of the underlined words.

Name _____

Add –s, –ies, or –es.
Write the new words to complete the sentences.

1. monkey_____ We saw _____ at the zoo.

2. fl(y)_____ My uncle _____ a plane.

3. fall_____ Bryan _____ down a lot.

4. box_____ Two _____ came in the mail.

5. stop_____ Sara _____ running.

6. bunn(y)_____ _____ live in the yard.

7. lunch_____ We ate our _____ outside.

8. wash_____ Dad _____ the car every week.

9. basket_____ Maria filled two _____ with eggs.

10. grass_____ Many kinds of _____ grow here.

 Directions In school, your child learned about the word endings *-s* or *-es*. Read the words and sentences with your child.

Name _____

Read the sentences.
Circle words that have an **–s** or **–es** ending in the sentences.
Write the word on the line. **Tell** what the word means.

HINT: When a consonant comes before a final *y*, the *y* changes to an *i* and before **es** is added.

1. This store sells film and cameras.   _____

2. I watch as Jeff reaches for the top shelf.   _____

3. Selena got glasses from the eye doctor.   _____

4. Strawberries are the best fruit.   _____

5. Bill relaxes by the pool all day.   _____

6. This city has many libraries.   _____

7. We went to a farm to buy fresh peaches.   _____

8. Jack presses his pencil into the paper.   _____

9. Anita finishes first in every race.   _____

10. Alex quits everything he starts.   _____

School + Home **Directions** In school, your child learned about the word endings *-s* and *-es* words. Ask your child to read the sentences to you and to tell you what the circled word means.

Name _____

Add **–s** or **–es** to the words in the boxes.
Choose the word to complete each sentence.
Write the word.

HINT: When a consonant comes before a final *y*, change the *y* to an *i* and add **es.**

galaxy	myth	recipe	waltz

1. Of all my mom's _____, her cherry pie is the best.

2. The science fiction book describes a man who travels between
_____.

3. The class learned about Greek _____ and legends.

4. Long ago, _____ were popular dances.

diminish	multiply	harness	graduate

1. Every day Ryan _____ his horse and goes for a ride.

2. To find the area of the rectangle, Ella _____ the width
times the height.

3. My cousin _____ from the junior high this spring.

4. The rain forest _____ in size every year.

 Directions Read each sentence with your child. Ask him or her to tell you what each word
means and how he or she knew to add *-s* or *-es*.

98 Word Endings *-s, -es*

Vocabulary Lesson 20

Add –ing and **–ed** to each word.
Write the words on the lines.

	ing	ed
1. cook	_____	_____
2. fish	_____	_____
3. snow	_____	_____
4. clos(e)	_____	_____
5. jump	_____	_____
6. rac(e)	_____	_____
7. rain	_____	_____
8. paint	_____	_____
9. play	_____	_____
10. rak(e)	_____	_____

School + Home **Directions** In school, your child learned about the word endings *-ing* or *-ed*. Read the words with your child. Then take turns using the words in sentences.

Name _____

Read the base word and sentences.
Add –ed to the base word to complete the first sentence.
Add –ing to the base word to complete the second sentence.

1. count

Today I _____ five different kinds of birds. I am

_____ birds for a school project.

2. smile

Alice _____ and looked away. Molly asked her what

she was _____ about.

3. chase

My dog _____ a squirrel. He loves

_____ things that move quickly.

4. complain

Bob _____ about the food, the music, and the movie.

Bob is always _____ about something.

5. flash

At the concert, the lights _____ brightly. You could see

them _____ from a mile away.

 Directions In school, your child learned about *-ed* and *-ing* endings. Ask your child to read the sentences to you. Then with your child think of other sentences that use these words.

Vocabulary Lesson 21

Name _____

Add –ed and **–ing** to the words in the boxes.
Choose the words to best complete the sentences.
Write the words.

| cancel | guide | recover | surround | challenge |

1. Last week, Lucy _____ Tara to a race. Tara said yes, but

beating Lucy will be very _____.

2. I used to get magazines in the mail, but today I _____

them. I am _____ my magazines so I do not waste paper.

3. Last year Mark hurt his arm and spent four months

_____. Now he is fully _____ and

can pitch again.

4. Years ago Rick _____ us up along the mountain trail.

This year Rick is _____ an entire tour group.

5. On the beach, Jack was _____ by soft white sand.

The _____ area was all beaches and blue water.

 Directions Read each sentence with your child. Ask him or her to tell you what each word means and how he or she knew to add *-ed* or *-ing*.

Name _____

Read the words.
Underline the homographs.
Circle the words that go with the picture.

1. taking a bow   tie a bow

2. live music   where we live

3. strong wind   roads that wind

4. sports fan   blowing fan

5. wake up   wake from a boat

6. today's date   eat a date

Directions In school, your child learned about homographs, or words that are spelled the same but have different meanings. Some homographs have different pronunciations. Read the phrases with your child. Then take turns saying what the homographs mean.

Name _____

Read the sentences.
Underline the homographs.
Circle the sentence that goes with the picture.

1. A good coach will never desert the team.

   Kathy walked in the desert sand.

2. Omar got a bicycle for a present.

   I want to present my story to the class.

3. Watch what the runner does.

   The does in the forest are beautiful to see.

4. The white dove landed on the tree branch.

   We all dove off the platform into the lake.

5. Rob turned up the bass on the radio.

   We ate the bass that Mike caught for dinner.

6. I am going to hide behind this tree.

   This purse was made from deer hide.

Directions In school, your child learned that homographs are words that have the same spelling but different meanings. Some homographs have different pronunciations. Ask your child to read the sentences to you. Then talk about the meaning of each homograph that is not pictured.

Name _____

Choose the homograph from the box that best completes each
sentence.
Write the word. Use each word twice.

buffet	conflict	entrance	content	loaf

1. World War II was the deadliest _____ in human history.

2. A crowd lined up outside the _____ to the theater.

3. At the bakery, we bought muffins and a _____ of bread.

4. The two witnesses in the trial have stories that _____.

5. Carol curled up in her bed and felt _____ to be home.

6. Today I want to just _____ and watch TV.

7. The actor tried to _____ the children with magic tricks.

8. Laura ate eggs and toast from the breakfast _____.

9. We watched the fierce winds _____ the shore.

10. Katie liked the book's _____, but not the pictures.

School + Home **Directions** Read each sentence with your child. Ask your child to tell you what each homograph means. Ask him or her to point out which homographs have different pronunciations.

104 Homographs

Vocabulary Lesson 22

Name _____

Put the words in alphabetical order.
Match the words to their definitions. **Use** a dictionary.

in•sects	flood	peb•ble	wheat	shel•ter	par•ent

1. | | flow of water over dry land |

2. | | very small animals with six legs |

3. | | a father or mother |

4. | | a small stone |

5. | | something that covers or protects you from weather or danger |

6. | | a grain used to make pasta and other food |

 Directions In school, your child learned that entry words in dictionaries are organized in alphabetical, or *ABC*, order. Read the words and definitions with your child. Then take turns thinking of sentences for each word.

Vocabulary Lesson 23

Dictionary, Glossary, and Thesaurus **105**

Name _____

Read the words and definitions.
Complete the sentences at the bottom by writing the entry word.
Write each sentence below the matching definition.

bar•ri•er, *NOUN*. something that stands in the way; something that stops progress or prevents movement:

| |
| |

mag•ni•fy, *VERB*.

1 to cause something to look larger than it really is:

| |
| |

2 to go beyond telling the truth in telling about something.

mar•gin, *NOUN*.

1 the blank space around the writing or printing on a page.

| |
| |

2 an extra amount.

vil•lain, *NOUN*. a very bad person:

| |
| |

At the end of the story, the _____ *was caught.*
The fence was a _____ *between the two houses.*
Please take notes in the _____ *of your paper.*
Use a microscope to _____ *the leaf.*

 Directions In school, your child learned about sentences and phrases in a dictionary that can help illustrate the meaning of a word. Read each word and definition with your child. Ask him or her to explain which sentence goes with which word.

Read the definitions.
Fill in the chart.

bal•lad (bal əd), *n.* **1** a simple song. **2** poem that tells a story in a simple verse form. Ballads are often sung. **3** a romantic popular song.

bi•og•ra•phy (bī og rə fē), *n.* an account of someone's life.

im•mi•grate (im ə grāt), *v.* to come into a country or region to live there: *Many people in Canada immigrated from Europe.*

per•pet•u•al (pər pech ü əl), *adj.* **1** never ceasing; continuous: *a perpetual stream of visitors*. **2** lasting forever; eternal: *the perpetual sky*.

Word	Pronunciation	Number of Syllables	Part of Speech
perpetual			
	(bal əd)		
		4	
			verb

Directions Read each word and definition with your child. Ask your child to tell you about all the different parts of a dictionary entry.

Name _____

Read each sentence.

Circle the context clue for the bold word or phrase.

1. Jan needs new school **supplies**, such as pencils and paper.

2. Kevin plays many **instruments**, including piano and violin.

3. We used plastic **utensils**, such as forks and spoons.

4. We need to put a **boundary**–for example a fence or a wall–between the dogs.

5. This store sells **technology**, like cell phones and computers.

6. Can you please wash the **linens**, including the sheets and towels?

7. This soup has a lot of **seasoning**, such as salt and pepper.

8. Lisa has lots of **camping equipment**, like tents and sleeping bags.

9. I have some new **furniture**, including a chair and a dresser, in my bedroom.

10. **Transportation**, such as planes, trains, and boats, changes over time.

 Directions In school, your child learned how an example can explain the meaning of a word or phrase in a sentence. Read each sentence with your child. Then take turns adding words or phrases to the example to make it clearer.

Name _____

Read the sentences.
Circle the clue words.
Underline the synonyms or antonyms.

1. The moon revolves around Earth, and Earth rotates around the Sun too.

2. E-mails transmit messages, and fax machines send messages too.

3. One room was radiant with light, but the other room was dim.

4. I thought the cake would taste terrible, but it tasted wonderful!

5. The air was so humid that the walls were damp.

6. The path was rugged, but the ground near the tents was smooth.

7. The news astounded my Dad, and it surprised the rest of the family too.

8. The movie is about a man who seems cowardly but turns out to be brave.

9. Jack will discuss the crisis, and he will talk about how to fix the problem too.

10. Mrs. Reese said she was happy, but her face looked displeased.

Directions In school, your child learned how to use synonyms or antonyms to figure out the meanings of a word in a sentence. Ask your child to read each sentence. Then help your child change a sentence so that it has antonyms instead of synonyms or vice versa.

Name _____

Read the sentences.
Match the bold word to its meaning.
Write the letter on the line.

_____ 1. Maria loves to buy fashion **accessories**, such as hats, belts, sunglasses, and necklaces.

_____ 2. The **aviator** put on his goggles and got into the small plane. The crowd cheered as he made the plane spin in the sky.

_____ 3. Derrick was **confident** that they would win the contest, but Emily felt unsure.

_____ 4. Julie's grandfather is a **robust** man who exercises every day. He built a new house last summer, and he did most of the work!

_____ 5. **Currency** in the U.S. is called *dollars*. In Canada, money is called *dollars* too.

a) a person who flies airplanes; pilot

b) strong and healthy

c) having a feeling you can do well or succeed

d) the money that a country uses

e) something added to something else to make it more attractive or useful

Directions Read each sentence with your child. Ask your child to tell you what kind of context clue helped him or her figure out the meaning of each bold word.

Vocabulary Lesson 24

Write each word with the added prefix or suffix.
Draw a line to the word's meaning.

1. dark **+ ish**

_____   plane in the air

2. small **+ est**

_____   not happy

3. un + happy

_____   a little bit dark

4. pre + cook

_____   the most small

5. air + plane

_____   yell now

6. fair **+ ly**

_____   cook before

7. yell **+ ing**

_____   in a fair way

School + Home

Directions In school, your child learned how to use word structure, or word parts, to figure out the meaning of a word. Ask your child to read each word. Then take turns using the words in sentences.

Name _____

Read the sentences.
Write the base word or words of each bold word.
Circle prefixes, suffixes, and word endings.

_____ **1.** Using an old map can **misdirect** you and take you to the wrong place.

_____ **2.** Sara seemed **unaware** of the dark clouds above her head.

_____ **3.** To Jacob, his cousin's house was the most **delightful** place in the world.

_____ **4.** Erin spread the icing **smoothly** over the top of the cake.

_____ **5.** The bear **blended** so well into the forest we could not see it.

_____ **6.** There was a blue car in the Smiths' **driveway** that Tasha had never seen before.

_____ **7.** Give me your address so I can send you a **postcard.**

 Directions In school, your child learned about word structure, or word parts. Ask your child to read the sentences and tell you the meaning of each bold word. Talk with your child about the word parts he or she found and what they mean.

Read the sentences.
Circle words with suffixes or prefixes. **Underline** words with word endings.
Put a box around compound words.
Write the words across from their meanings.

1. Jon used a slingshot to get the ball out of the tree.

2. Right now Becky is slumbering on the beach.

3. My sister was misinformed about the time of our show, so she came late.

4. Alicia has to reweave part of her basket for art class.

5. Mrs. Jones felt sorrowful as she drove away from the house.

_____   full of sadness

_____   sleeping

_____   given wrong information

_____   stick used to shoot small stones

_____   remake by crossing threads

Directions Ask your child to read the sentences and tell you about the word parts of the words he or she marked. Ask your child to say the meaning of each word in his or her own words.